NOBODY KNOWS
I'M FAMOUS

Thank You
11/4/17
9:35pm

Also by Shawn Persinger

Halloween Baptizm (Portfolio)
I'm An Alligator. I'm A Crocodile.
The 50 Greatest Guitar Books
The Uncommon Guitar Lesson
Desire for a Straight Line (Portfolio)
The Art of Modern Primitive Guitar (Portfolio)
The Young Person's Guide to Free Improvisation & Experimental Music

NOBODY KNOWS I'M FAMOUS

A Year In The Life Of An Unknown Musician

SHAWN PERSINGER

Illustrated by Gonzalo Fuentes

Publisher: Quixotic Music
Editor and proofreader: Anne Schmidt
Cover Art: *Modern Primitive Melodies* by Gonzalo Fuentes

Contents © 2017 Shawn Persinger

Library of Congress Cataloging-in-Publication Data

Persinger, Shawn
Nobody Knows I'm Famous
ISBN# 9781548645557

Contents (Essays)

Acknowledgements

I am grateful beyond measure for the help and support of the following friends and acquaintances who contributed to the creation of this book. Anne Schmidt for tireless edits, revisions, suggestions, and moral support; Jim Kirlin, Erika Haskell, Katherine Thurman, Brian Slattery, Thom Guthrie, Tom Schulte, Joanne Thompson, and Joe Casillo for reading early drafts and excerpts; Dr. Robert Zatorre for my answering my questions regarding the brain's response to music; Jack Vees, Del Rey, Steve Feigenbaum, and Matthieu Brouillard for providing professional and artistic perspective; my various students who inspired some of the essays; Hank Hoffman for triggering my "Bernstein epiphany"; Wang Ao for China and much more; Bill Fischer and Anna Marra for inviting me to be part of the BMAD documentary; The Luck Pushers, Emily B., and the Running On Empty band for insisting I show off; Soften The Glare for being even better than I had hoped for; my guitars; Jim T. and Diane S. Lestor for believing in the entire *Halloween* project; Claudia and Atticus Persinger for inspiration; and my parents, Calvin and Judy Persinger for everything else.

And a very special thanks to Gonzalo Fuentes for clever, playful, and perceptive artwork that went above and beyond my expectations.

INTRODUCTION

The Plan And The Tangents

I kept this diary because it seems most audiences rarely see or hear about the operose, serendipitous, and Gordian work that goes into creating a piece of contemporary music – dare I say a piece of "art". In my case, I am talking about *Halloween Baptizm* (which I'll get to later).

Of course, the interested reader will find plenty of musician's autobiographies, critical analyses (usually from the third person point of view), and documentaries about classic rock albums, but these are always looking back, not chronicling the moment. Chronicling the moment is what I tried to do here.

But rereading the diary, I noticed that there were plenty of musical/artistic/creative tangents, crossing streams of consciousness, which I was compelled to follow. It seems I seldom get from point **A** to point **B** without visiting any number of other points in-between. These tangents make up a considerable part of the diary.

Expurgations

This diary has been heavily abridged. I took out most references to band rehearsals, teaching events, books I read, films I watched, my (almost) daily meditation and walks, and gigs – anything that had little relevance to the creation of *Halloween Baptizm* or my thoughts on music in general.

I also took out almost all references to my family: One early reader commented, "The familial references are like interruptions from another room: literary equivalents to, 'Dad, can you come here for a minute?'"

Opinions Are Like...

In January of 2016 I began teaching *The History of Rock* at the University of New Haven*. On the first day of class I let my students know that our examination of rock and roll would be focusing on historical facts (as many as can be gleaned from the dubious mythology of rock and roll), music theory, and the understanding and practical use of aesthetic vocabulary. However, in addition to those objective approaches, we would also pursue investigations of music and art that do not lead to definitive conclusions. Some inquires would be more akin to a *Zen Kōan* – an "unanswerable" question, to be meditated upon and replied to thoughtfully whether or not there is a definitive answer. In our class we would contemplate such questions – particularly those regarding opinion and taste – in order to invoke judicious responses, rather than answer them as true or false.

---

* The History of Rock class is one of the art appreciation – "Aesthetic Responsiveness" – options offered at the University of New Haven. Description from the course catalogue: "Study of rock music as a musical tradition and social, political, and economic phenomenon. Ethnomusicological and historical examination of rock from its pre-1955 roots to the present."

I went on to tell the students that, by virtue of my age, I have had more experiences than they, but that their experiences are most likely different than mine. Consequently, unless they only wanted the opinion of a 45-year-old, straight, white, middle-class male from the suburbs they would need to speak up: Because, while I do believe my opinions are open-minded and well-researched, many of my judgments and, most importantly, my experiences, would not be the same as theirs. Hence, I encouraged the voicing of students' opinions and preferences as they would supplement and enhance the course.

This book is not my class. Other outlooks are not mine to provide. I make no apology for this; I point it out so that readers are aware that I am cognizant of my limited perspective and that all of my opinions should be – like all opinions – understood in context.

The Ostensible Essays

This diary has documented the work at hand, the day-to-day activities I was engaged in, and thoughts that were born out of them. Thus the titled essays are in fact merely daily entries that ended up being relatively extensive, as well as focused enough to warrant headings.

As a result, while many of the titled pieces are reflective and, to a small degree, analytical, they were also spontaneous, which means some of them might be naïve and some may contradict others. I have no problem with this. I am not running for political office and I have no reason or desire to be dogmatic; in fact, my point of view is persuadable. That is not to say I don't have fundamental personal values, but I am open to a reasoned and thoughtful differing of opinion. Hence, the ostensible essays were not written to proselytize, but rather to provide food for thought.

Furthermore, during this diary's creation I read several books on contemporary music practices and theories written with the scholarly method – *File Under Popular* by Chris Cutler and *Pop Into Art* by Simon Frith and Howard Horne, to name but two I particularly enjoyed. And though I do appreciate a highly analytical perspective, I dislike having to weed through formalized language that, while attempting to construct a precise text with no possibility of misinterpretation, ironically makes the subject matter more difficult to understand! Consequently, I purposely avoided such a didactic approach – it's a diary for goodness sake! It's homespun. At best this diary embraces simplicity without being simple. At its worst it's naïve without, hopefully, appearing foolish.

APRIL

NOBODY KNOWS I'M FAMOUS

I'm working under the premise that if I write half a page a day for the next year, I'll produce a publishable manuscript that illuminates the inner workings of *Halloween Baptizm* and my thoughts on music in general. This suggests the possible fallacy that people – normal people *and* musicians – will be interested in what I have to say. This is one of the problems of being a relatively unknown musician: The presumption that your work and ideas are of interest to others *and* possess intrinsic value even though you've not been able to turn that work or those ideas into substantial renown or monetary income. Let me be more forthright and specific:

The presumption that *my* work and ideas are of interest to others and possess intrinsic value even though *I've* not been able to turn that work or those ideas into substantial renown or monetary income.

Splendid, I can work with these presumptions, as most people don't seem to know who *anybody* is!

24 April 2016, Sunday

Constructive *Halloween* work has been accomplished the past two days – composing (revising really), arranging, formatting notation, and practicing the parts. With that, I suppose I should elaborate on *Halloween Baptizm*.

HALLOWEEN BAPTIZM
Part I: Origins

In 2003 I spent two weeks at the Fundacion Valparasio artist retreat in Almeria, Spain. Most of my time was spent blissfully floundering through Stravinsky and Bernstein scores – *The Firebird Suite* and *The Symphonic Dances of West Side Story*, respectively – trying to glean composition and arranging insight. I also worked my way through Walter Everett's indispensable, two-volume *The Beatles as Musicians*, and wrote one solo guitar piece, "Gray Green Yellow" (the title of which reflects the autumn landscape of Almeria).

I came home inspired: So much so that I recorded my album *The Art of Modern Primitive Guitar* [see Appendix II] in two days. Motivated by the quick completion of that recording, I set myself the quixotic task of writing one new piece of music every day for the month of November, though the first one was written on October 31, thus *Halloween Baptizm* (the spelling of "Baptizm" is a nod to the Art Ensemble of Chicago album *Bap-Tizum*). Unfortunately, my ambition outweighed my motivation; I barely managed 12 new pieces and that included carrying the project into December.

Still, the 12 pieces were good. They were also unorthodox, as I had composed them not for specific instrumentation but for musical registers – the relative "height" or range of a set of pitches for any given instrument, such as the most commonly known vocal types, soprano, tenor, baritone, and bass. Consequently, the music could be played with an almost infinite combination of instruments.

I notated the *Halloween* pieces in the computer program Finale, imported the notation into the recording program Logic, created some rough mixes using virtual instrument sounds, and then, having no immediate outlet for the music, set them aside. And there they sat, on my computer, for almost 12 years.

Part II: The 8-String Baritone Etudes
(A Brief Digression)

In August 2015 I decided (the Muse suggested) to try and complete a different ongoing music project (one unrelated to *Halloween*) – my 8-String Baritone Etudes.

I first played a Taylor 8-string baritone guitar in January of 2010, at the Taylor Guitars' factory in El Cajon, CA. [For the sake of brevity the 8-string baritone will henceforth be abbreviated as "8".] As I played it I thought, "This instrument is fantastically odd and impractical...it's perfect for me!" But it cost $3,000, which was unviable for me at the time, so I wistfully let it go.

However, in 2013 I sold my house and, surprisingly, there was a little bit of money left over. I took the remainder and bought wooden window blinds for my new home (perhaps the most sensible adult purchase I've ever made – what I had really wanted was a candy-apple-red Gibson SG) and I ordered myself an "8".

When the guitar arrived several months later, it was everything I had hoped for. With gargantuan bottom strings more suitable for a bass and two pairs of octave strings (like a 12-string) where one would normally find the two middle strings, the instrument was sumptuous – strumming an *E* chord was like warm chocolate pudding for your ears. But it was also perplexing, stroppy, and unforgiving – with all due respect, the guitar is basically three obtusely designed two-stringed instruments crammed onto one fretboard. I loved it! [For technical notes on the "8" see Appendix I: The 8-String Baritone]

I immediately decided that I would write music specifically for this obstreperous instrument, approaching it the way composers of the 18th century had to approach the piano after years of writing for the harpsichord. The "8" looks like a guitar but it is not. And while one can play traditional guitar styles on the "8" (like playing harpsichord music on a piano), why would you? The "8" had something different to offer. The problem was, what? This I hoped to figure out.

Beginning in earnest in December of 2013, I completed two pieces within a few days of acquiring the "8". It became evident to me that these pieces, though self-standing cohesive musical works, could also serve as etudes that would exploit the aberrant features of the "8" – the low tuning, the massive overtones that bellow from open-strings and harmonics, the seemingly unbounded sustain and glacial decay, the divergent octave strings in the middle of the fretboard, the sympathetic vibration of unmuted open-strings (which can be burdensome but can also be used for effect), and more.

Straightaway I was reminded of Leo Brouwer's *20 Estudios Sencillos (20 Simple Etudes)*, which are profound in their unrivaled balance of musical elegance and technical practicality. My second thought was of the simplest etudes of Sor and Caracassi; such pieces as the literally titled

"Andantino" and "Waltz in G". These are beginner etudes, which are fairly easy to play but also sound like "real music". Pieces such as these are some of the most challenging to compose – if they were easy to write more of them would exist. Using these composers and their etudes as models, I now had a framework within which to compose short, stylized pieces for the "8" that would be character driven rather than technically driven: Technique *would* be required but only in service of this magnificent and unruly character.

The first two etudes arrived from the Muse with grace – like unassuming gifts fitted in boxes with simple, handmade bows. I sincerely believed they wanted – they needed – to be written. And then, as quickly as the first two had come, others deferred. I didn't worry. I kept playing the "8", experimenting with different approaches, employing some so-called "avant-garde" techniques that are hardly new but are uncommon, and also playing "normal" guitar music that, frankly, the "8" didn't seem interested in pursuing. And then, just like with *Halloween*, I set the etudes aside.

Part III: I Stockpile And I Wait

Intermittently, "I stockpile and I wait" has been a mantra of mine. As it happens, for better or for worse, I get excited by a musical project – such as Boud Deun, Modern Primitive Guitar, *Halloween*, Prester John (my acoustic duo with mandolinist David Miller), or the "8" – and I compose for it prolifically. After composing, if there are the means – an outlet such as a band to perform the music; funding to help with the expenses of recording, manufacturing, and touring (composing fringe guitar music doesn't normally generate significant income); or the unrelenting desire to give a solo performance – I bring the music to the public. More often than not, I stockpile and I wait.

I know this is not an advantageous work ethic: As Chuck Close has attested, "Inspiration is for amateurs. The rest of us just show up for work."* And I agree with this. But what is the "work"?

In the examples of *Halloween* and the 8-string Baritone etudes, the work is the composing, and I show up for that job as often as the Muse calls me. But there is additional work to be done – learning the music, obtaining funding for production, performing, recording, marketing, distributing, booking the shows, etc. – and that work may or may not be my job. This is a dilemma of many contemporary musicians: How can one do so many jobs and be good at any of them? So, when it comes to composing, I show up, do the work, and then…I stockpile and I wait.**

And wait I did.

Then, unexpectedly, in the spring of 2016 the wait was over.

Part IV: Maturation

In March of 2016 I received an email from my editor at *Wood&Steel* proposing that I write an article on the merits of the "8". I responded enthusiastically, suggesting that I could work something up that would speak to current 8-string owners as well as the curious. And with that, after a two-year hiatus, I was once again seriously interested in the "8".

---

* "Arts as Antidote for Academic Ills" Patricia Cohen *The New York Times* December 18, 2012

** I don't just sit around and do nothing while I wait. I teach; perform other music; make instructional videos; write books, articles, and lessons; practice; read; I even keep composing new music.

I played my etudes and found them as enchanting as ever. But, I knew that these pieces were not for the everyday guitarist. They were (are), for lack of a better word, "arty". And I know that arty is not necessarily everyone's taste, certainly not that of the majority. So I needed to tailor my article to speak to the most practical and general aspects of the "8", and, if it was possible without being pushy or conceited, I would also mention my more grandiose plans.

My editor approved my outline so I started writing. Then something miraculous happened: synchronicity. I received, out of the blue, an email from a complete stranger with the subject header, "Music for Taylor 8-String Baritone". It read:

I'm looking for music that is suited for the lower register of the Taylor 8-string Baritone. I found one piece that fits the request, "Justify" from the Whalebone album Runes, *but I am looking for more. Have you written any? Thanks for helping.*

This was a peculiar concurrence as no one but myself, my editor, and a few people at Taylor Guitars knew I was writing the article on the "8". I responded to this gentleman's email cordially, if conditionally:

Yes I do have some music written for the 8-string, but it is not commercially available. However, since you've asked...

My pieces follow in the tradition of the artistic etudes of J.S. Bach's The Well-Tempered Clavier; *Leo Brouwer's* Estudios Sencillos; *and even John Cage's* Sonatas and Interludes for Prepared Piano. *These pieces are a combination of etude, experiment, and (if I may be so bold) Art. I am holding out on a commercial release until there is proper funding to make the project a success on multiple levels. Does that make me sound like a selfish artist?*

I hope you'll stay in touch. If the etudes become viable you'll be one of the first to know.

I'll cut to the chase: After a few more emails in which we discussed my various artistic goals, this gentleman, along with his wife, offered to help fund the completion of not only the 8-string Baritone etudes but also a recording of *Halloween Baptizm* for an uncommon acoustic guitar quartet I had been formulating – nylon-string, 6-string, 8-string baritone, and 12-string. The commercial release* of this music would be titled *Halloween Baptizm* and include 13 *Halloween* pieces (I'd have to compose one more, I only had 12 so far) and at least four 8-string baritone etudes. In addition to the recorded music, I also planned to publish a portfolio book of notated scores, with composition and performance notes. A few days later I decided that I would try to keep this diary documenting the entire creative process and, if it was half interesting or could be useful to others, publish it as well.

A few weeks later I received a check from my patrons**, started this diary, swiftly composed one new etude, and completed a second one that had been left unfinished for more than two years. And so it goes that money can't buy you love, or happiness, or peace of mind, but if you already have those things, money can help in a multitude of other ways. And as I have come to learn, the history of art and music is filled with stories such as mine…so here we are. Although, one last detail remains:

---

* The release is scheduled for October 31st, 2017. This relatively distant deadline was a circumspect strategy on my part (a rare one) as I presumed that between my regular teaching schedule, my new position at the university, and life in general, a copious amount of time would be required to fulfill all the requirements – composing, recording, mixing, commissioning the artwork and design, manufacturing, etc. – of the project.

** After the commission had been offered, I contacted The American Composers Forum (ACF), who facilitated the funding by way of a program called "Fiscal Sponsorship", which allows individual donors to provide tax-deductible arts funding to specific individuals.

I have struggled with the dilemma of whether or not to disclose the dollar amount that the commission granted me.

One brings up the topic of money and it comes across as either crass or naïve. Yet money is significant and I think the particulars could be useful to others artists. Therefore, this is something I am willing to discuss in-person, but am reticent to share in print. However, I will state that the dollar amount was enough to fund roughly 75% of the projected production costs of *Halloween*.

25 April 2016, Monday

Even though I should be working on *Halloween*, this morning I recorded two new pieces for *Regarding Gravity*, a film that my friend Matthieu Brouillard has written, directed, and produced*. I met Matthieu (who, in addition to being a filmmaker, is an artist and photographer) almost 20 years ago while traveling in Morocco. We have been hoping to do a project together ever since. I've been working on the soundtrack, piecemeal, for about a year. Matthieu is currently in the final stages of post-production so he needed new music from me today. I suspect more pieces will be composed and finalized in the coming weeks.

Working on the soundtrack has been a pleasure as Matthieu's film is beguiling and recondite, and the Muse has held my hand through the entire process. I've recorded approximately two hours of music but I suspect Matthieu won't use more than 30 minutes worth. Thus far it has been guitar-based, primarily acoustic, although there are two electric themes – one hallucinatory, the other fractious. I've also used the "8" for many of the pieces, which has been a nice break from the formal structures of the etudes. And though the soundtrack

---

* For more, visit www.RegardingGravity.com

has distracted me from working on *Halloween*, most of Matthieu's pieces are short variations on three themes I composed early on – and once I get a good theme, creating a variation is invigorating – so the process has been more play than work. There is an indefinite plan to release the recordings, used and unused, on a soundtrack CD, *Music For And Inspired By* Regarding Gravity.

26 April 2016, Tuesday

After practicing my 8-string baritone "Etude No. 3" for the twentieth time today, the Muse offered up a marvelous new variation – an octave displacement waltz. Each of the three beats, in every measure, gets the same note, but in different octaves and on different strings, working through the sequence *A-C-B-D-F-E-G-A*. It's amusingly cumbersome to perform as it incorporates massive leaps up and down the fingerboard, but, because it's in 3/4, it floats and swirls like a heroine in a Jane Austen novel.

27 April 2016, Wednesday

Today I heard one of my old songs, "Good King Friday" on the Frank Zappa Pandora station. That was gratifying. Although…

In the 1990s I was in a progressive/fusion band (with understated punk influences) called, regrettably, Boud Deun. My number one piece of advice to young musicians: Name your band something people can easily spell and pronounce. Even something cliché – though you should give it a twist: How many awful hippie-jam-bands were called "Nirvana" before 1989? Boud Deun is one of the worst band names ever and possibly the most baffling professional/artistic mistake I have ever made. That band was something special and I'm sure we would have sold many more records if we had been called "Good King Friday", which was one of the names in the running when we voted on it.

29 April 2016, Friday

Finished my latest article/lesson for ReverbLessons.com this morning, "Country Guitar for the Rock Guitarist." That should be posted in a couple of weeks.

For the most part, the articles I write for bigger outlets – *Premier Guitar*, ReverbLessons.com, *Wood&Steel* – are decidedly mainstream. Though there have been a few exceptions. For instance, last December *Premier Guitar* published my John McLaughlin and the Mahavishnu Orchestra "electric etude". The etude was supplemented with a recording I made, featuring a complex McLaughlin-esque arpeggio pattern, angular melody, and frenetic solo (I'm extraordinarily fond of the solo I recorded, it sounds like a McLaughlin outtake from *Inner Mounting Flame*, an album I devoured in my early 20s). But the lesson received no feedback from readers whatsoever! Goodness knows that site must do traffic in the millions, yet one of the best articles I've ever written fell on deaf ears.

Conversely, the next lesson I wrote for *Premier Guitar* was titled "How 'Freebird' Taught Me Everything I Need to Know About Rock Guitar Soloing" – pure clickbait (though the lesson does have genuine value). What happened? Feedback galore!

"Freebird" and Lynyrd Skynyrd, everyone's got an opinion; John McLaughlin and the Mahavishnu Orchestra, not so much.

At 44 years old, this is still something I struggle with: Why do the majority of people ignore so many wondrous and unconventional artistic creations? (I could list specific artists but this diary will doubtlessly be filled with their names.) Part of me hopes that my daily entries might help to:

❖ Provide a credible, non-cynical answer to the above question.

❖ Provide an answer to *why* I need to know an answer to the above question.

❖ Provide release from the need to know an answer, because, perhaps, no answer is possible.

30 April 2016, Saturday

The Muse, the Divine source, the oneness of all things – how silly it all sounds, like a superstition or ghost story or New Age mumbo jumbo. The cynic in me recoils when I read mawkish and overly precious descriptions of transcendent artistic experiences. But I get it. I understand it. I believe it. I experience it daily.

Nevertheless, I feel slightly embarrassed when I talk about it. It? "Artistic Spirituality" if you will. So when I do bring "It" up, I clarify that, "I know this sounds ludicrous. If someone had said this to me ten years ago I too would have rolled my eyes superciliously. I also know that it can come across as sophomoric or even worse, phony."

But it's all true! There is a Muse, a divine source, and a oneness of all things!

Still, trying to describe these sanctified entities with too much reverence seems to diminish their importance. Yes, they are sublime but they are also so ubiquitous as to be analogous to air or water. And as I don't write about my daily intake of those vital and life-sustaining forces, I will therefore limit any detailed discussion of the divine source, which I encounter on a regular basis, to *this* sole entry – with the understanding that I acknowledge the Muse daily and with immense gratitude.

MAY

SCIENCE AND SUPERSTITION

There are four major conceptual themes that run throughout *Halloween* – science, mathematics, superstition, and an oversimplification of their relationship. I am eager to stress this oversimplification for two reasons: 1) I know very little about science, math, or superstition (folk tradition, ritual implications, etc.) and 2) an oversimplification allows me as an artist – not a scientist, folklorist, sociologist, or ethnographer – to offer talking points, without judgment, which allows the audience to form their own opinions.

My lack of understanding aside, I do know that these subjects are fraught with ambiguity, paradox, and the unknowable. This is exciting to me, particularly the unknowable. It's okay not to know. But it's not okay to not know that you don't know! I know I don't know, and that's okay.

Thematic parameters for naming all the *Halloween* pieces:

- ❖ All titles will begin with numbers, such as, "Two Is The First Sophia Germain Prime", "Three Hundred Years Of A Hypothetical Moon", etc.

- ❖ There can be subtitles, e.g.: "One Zero: Periodic Orbits From Chaos To Order And Back".

- ❖ Title or subtitle should relate either to the celebration of Halloween (or cultural variations)*, superstitions, mathematics, or some sort of scientific theory, fact, or practice.

I see science and superstition as attractive and intriguing opposite ends of a spectrum. One could substitute other juxtapositions, Reality-Imagination, Fact-Fiction, True-False, Real-Fake, but one facet I particularly like about the Science-Superstition relationship is that science has proven some superstitions to be true (we just don't call them superstitions anymore), and can thus be seen as a vocation that attempts to *disprove* as much as it tries to prove. So in some ways these two disparate worldviews are related. Ultimately I think this is what it means to keep an open mind – acknowledging both sides of any story, embracing contradictions, and still managing to function productively (and hopefully for the betterment of life). Additionally, one of the appeals of Halloween is that most people recognize it as a holiday of superstitions and have fun with it, as opposed to superstitions people truly believe in, which can be rife with pitfalls.

---

* My favorite explanation of the origin of Halloween is that it derives from the Celtic festival of Samhain, which was celebrated at the end of the fall harvest. According to Celtic mythology, around this time of year the division between reality and the "Otherworld" diminishes and spirits become more active; thus my use of the word "superstition".

These notions of contradiction are ones I've played with for many years. They are the basis of what "Modern Primitive Guitar" and "Modern Primitive Acoustic Scientist Music" means to me. Sure those are catchy names (are they?) but they also carry meaning. Music is very much the art...perhaps I can substitute the word "magic" for "superstition" here. Music is the art of magic and science. The magic is the inspiration, the conjuring of something that didn't exist before, the gift from the Muse. The science is the actual work of physically and aurally manifesting that magic.

2 May 2016, Monday

Although this diary focuses on my music and work routine, I feel the need to explain my personal time with my kids.

I have two children, one of each, five and seven. My ex-wife and I have joint custody. My kids stay with me overnight an average of three nights a week. One additional afternoon I pick them up from school, we do activities (games, dance party, or music jams – my kids are adept at jamming; you wouldn't call what we play a "song" but it is definitely music), and have dinner together. So I'm with my kids typically four to five days a week. They are a huge part of my daily life. They have also bolstered my creativity, inspiring me with their clever verbal propensities and artistic pursuits (my daughter is an inventive illustrator of flying cats and surreal landscapes; and my son is an enthusiastic model builder, from both blueprints and his own imagination).

But when I started this diary I decided to omit my daily activities with them so as to keep my family life private; avoid exaggerating the struggles of the being an artist *and* a parent – they are no more difficult than the struggles *every* parent faces; and because I am the cliché bragging, hyperbolizing, cloying caricature of an overly zealous father. My kids are marvelous! But do you really want to read that on every page?

4 May 2016, Wednesday

Feeling optimistic. I just finished working on *Halloween* "One...", applying an idea I've had for some time: That music should always be, on some level, danceable. I don't unremittingly accept this as true – I'm never dogmatic – but it's a principle I'm currently working with.

Dance music engages the body in a way that much "art", "listening", or "concert" music doesn't. *Halloween* is arty; it is listening music. But, if I can underlay danceable grooves in the pieces – even if they're subliminal – then I might have something slightly new to offer fans of arty listening music. Maybe I can reach some dance music people too.

Consequently, today I searched for a way to perform the more abstract pieces of *Halloween* over dance grooves, which I'll eventually make invisible. I started by creating some drum loops from a variety of funk and hip hop samples. Then, experimenting with the syncopated melody of "One...", I tried to fit it into a 4/4 dance groove. Originally the piece was full of mixed meters, 6/8 - 3/8 - 4/8, but that was for notation purposes. Today I took about 30 minutes to retranscribe the chart into 2/4, which not only makes it more legible but more importantly syncs it up with the drum loop. The melody is still absurdly rhythmically complicated (it's reminiscent of Zappa's "Black Page") but now it frolics on top of a funky drumbeat!

5 May 2016, Thursday

Just spent a decent 15 minutes working on "Everybody Have Fun Tonight" by Wang Chung, as an 80s cover band I play with has it in their set list. 15 minutes might not seem like much, but we've been playing this song for almost a year and I've spent time with it before, so a quarter of an hour seems like a lot to me. Why am I doing it? Why do I, a professional musician whose appetite leans towards the fringe and the uncommercial (King Crimson, The Mahavishnu Orchestra, Nomeansno, Leo Kottke, The Minutemen) play in a mainstream '80s cover band that doesn't make much money and takes up my time practicing and rehearsing? Easy: I like the music, it *can* be fun, and maybe I'll learn something. For instance:

I long ago concluded that "Everybody Have Fun Tonight" was a dumb lyric, and thus I thought it was a dumb song in general. Nevertheless, in the spirit of keeping an open mind, I reluctantly agreed to learn it. It turns out that, the chorus lyrics aside, it's a first-rate piece of music! Distinctive guitar chord voicings for the verse, funky fills in the chorus, interesting harmonic movement in the bridge, and a second instrumental bridge that allows room for improvisation. Those are admirable qualities for a song: I'm happy to add any such tune to my repertoire.

But I won't play songs I don't respect. Though I did try it twice with the '80s band, but after two gigs I couldn't handle it. One of the songs we played is by a female-fronted group and has self-deprecating lyrics (written by a man) that make the singer appear to be a ditzy secretary-cum-teenybopper. The other song is by a band with a huge catalogue of fantastic new wave tunes from the early '80s yet we were playing one of their worst – plodding, formulaic, trite, void of any substance excepting a catchy (though vapid) chorus designed for the lowest common denominator. I insisted these two songs be removed from the setlist. They were. Integrity intact.

6 May 2016, Friday

Discovered the title for *Halloween* "Nine..." this morning – "The Ninth Day Of The Ninth Month". I say "discovered" because I know these titles exist in the realm of *Halloween*; I simply need to find them. I'll explain:

In *The KLF: Chaos, Magic and the Band Who Burned a Million Pounds* John Higgs judiciously writes how reality is brimming with infinite connections. Accordingly, with a little research and a lot of editing, anyone with a predetermined path can connect any two seemingly disparate events to create a plausible narrative, support a hypothesis, or build a conspiracy theory. Similarly, I recognized a long time ago that I would find serendipitous connections between the holiday of Halloween and the numbers 1-13 that would provide me with numerated titles for the pieces in *Halloween*. And it's working.

The Double Ninth Festival is a Chinese holiday that is observed on *the ninth day of the ninth month* of the Chinese calendar. On this day descendants pay homage to their deceased ancestors. This holiday is distinct from another Chinese festival that I discovered in my Halloween research, one called "The Hungry Ghost Festival", in which ghosts and spirits visit the living. So, while The Hungry Ghost Festival is more akin to Halloween, "The Ninth Day Of The Ninth Month" is more apropos for my needs. Still, the title "The Hungry Ghost" holds infinite charm, perhaps I can use it somewhere else [Note: I did, see 25 August 2016].

7 May 2016, Saturday

I find that using Salvador Dali's trick of working in 15-minute increments is extremely helpful in regard to urging me into action. Dali makes several references to this method in *Diary Of A Genius*, such as: "I live from one ten minutes to the next, savouring them one by one and transforming the quarters of an hour into battles won, into feats and spiritual victories." [p. 51]

I make no claims to Dali-esque accomplishments but once I began working in 15-minute increments I started to achieve more than I thought possible. Thus, my timer has been set.

• • •

Today I'm practicing for an upcoming benefit concert at which *Sgt. Pepper's Lonely Hearts Club Band* will be performed in its entirety. I'm excited by this opportunity. Playing the music of The Beatles must be differentiated from playing other cover tunes, it's more akin to a classical performance, a classical performance with a rock attitude – mistakes are acceptable, as long as there is energy and you genuinely know your parts. I know mine. At least I think I do – but then I'll hear previously undetected subtleties. For instance: Did you know that during the second chorus in "Fixing A Hole" – *"See the people standing there who disagree and never win and wonder why they don't get in my door."* – there are background vocals that go "dee-dee-dee-dee…do"? I didn't! Astonishing!

In addition to *Sgt. Pepper's*, all of *Led Zeppelin III* is also to be learned for yet another benefit. I've decided just now that I'm done learning cover songs for at least a year (not counting student requests). I love learning new songs, it's one of my favorite things to do, but in the past six months I have memorized and performed no less than 60 cover tunes! That's a fruitful learning experience, but goodness knows I couldn't be doing any of them justice in performance. After these two benefit concerts, *Halloween*, I'm all yours!

10 May 2016, Tuesday

Spent the last hour adding new parts to *Halloween* "Midnight" (the twelfth, and penultimate, piece in *Halloween*). This is a repetitive but staggered composition wherein it is difficult to immediately recognize the repetition. Until today it was scored for two voices but in the last 60 minutes I added a harmony to the melody, doubled the riff up an octave, and rearranged the parts, letting the 12-string spearhead the melody. I did all this using my "danceable listening music" method [see 4 May 2016], but this time with a thunderous, John Bonham-esque groove. At the risk of sounding like someone who doesn't know his metal from his METAL! – "Twelve" is the heavy metal character in *Halloween*.

11 May 2016, Wednesday

The Luck Pushers (another band of mine) played a "Swing, Rock & Roll, Honky Tonk, Sock Hop Dance Party" last night. As fun as that sounds, the gig was little more than fine, with lackluster attendance numbers and merely a tolerable performance from all band members, including myself.

The Luck Pushers only gig about once a month, which is not enough to get better than good. This is regrettable, because the band has potential, the fans that do attend our shows love us, and we get to play a tremendously fulfilling range of music. At last night's dance we played everything from Louis Prima to Tammy Wynette, Bob Wills to Chuck Berry, The Beatles (always The Beatles) to Tom T. Hall. There is also plenty of room for tasteful guitar virtuosity. And, unlike the other cover bands I play with, The Luck Pushers rarely stick to a setlist and are liable to improvise upon or extend the length of any given song at a moment's notice (though we sound nothing like the Grateful Dead, their spirit of free play is prevalent in a Luck Pushers show). Regretfully, since we don't play that much, we are rarely as exceptional as we could be.

I believe one of the reasons bands were better in the "old days" is because they gigged more. I recently watched the Twisted Sister documentary, *We Are Twisted F***ing Sister!*, which showed that those guys were earning a living by playing the NJ/NY bar scene five nights a week back in the 1970s!

And they were just one of dozens (hundreds?) of bands doing that. I can barely gig twice a month. No blame, no judgment, no longing for "the good old day", purely details of past vs. current circumstances.

One could argue that an explanation for why none of my current musical projects have been overly successful is because I'm spreading myself too thin, playing in too many bands, and playing too many diverse styles. I would agree with this except for the fact that I spent many years solely focused on one project at a time, Boud Deun (1994-1999), solo (1999-2004), and Prester John (2007-2015). Even given full-time attention, those endeavors were less successful than I thought they would have been. At the very least, this current approach of diversity keeps things fresh and keeps me busy.

13 May 2016, Friday

Today is Friday the 13th; it should be a promising day for work on *Halloween*. For whatever reason, I think of Friday the 13th – and the number 13 in general – as auspicious. Perhaps it's my desire to turn generally accepted negative ideas – especially superstitions – into positives. Berry Gordy Jr. wrote about this in his autobiography *To Be Loved*. (Gordy is the founder of Motown Records and wrote many of the label's biggest hits). Regarding the alchemy of turning negatives into positives, Gordy writes about calling one of his production teams at Motown "The Clan", reclaiming that word for the betterment of mankind. I love that.

13 is also a conceptual theme in *Halloween*. The Halloween-13 connection appears evident to me: Halloween is dark, scary, foreboding, etc. – 13 holds similar connotations for many people. And how magnificent is this: Halloween is on Oct. 31st – 31 and 13 are numerical palindromes! (I don't believe in numerology, but I like palindromes.) Thus, there are 13

pieces in *Halloween* – although I have only composed 12 pieces so far; the 13th is gestating.

• • •

Spent a solid hour working on "Eight Queens On An Imaginary Chess Board". It's been difficult to find the right key for this *Halloween* piece because I have been experimenting with the main motif in harmonics. *F#-E-G* works with natural harmonics but because of the perpetual motion (the phrase is played continuously for more than two minutes) the motif is difficult to perform steadily throughout. *A-G-Bb* works if I tune the second string down a half step, but the perpetual motion continues to be an issue. Finally, *E-D-F* also works, once again with the second string tuned down, but it is still challenging – almost impossible for me – to play. I'm considering other options.

14 May 2016, Saturday

A huge breakthrough on *Halloween* "Eight…" this morning: I'll play the main motif on the 12-string, with the top two strings – normally unison *E E* – tuned *B E*. This way I can play the motif as unisons on the third and fourth strings, and then I can move the motif to the first and second strings so it harmonizes in fourths. This is promising!

TO BE OR NOT TO BE (A ROCK STAR)?

I can't shake this desire that I've had all my life – to be a ROCK STAR! Why? If I had fulfilled this desire would I enjoy it? Can I replace it? What exactly do I wish for?

These questions were born (reborn, because I ask them frequently) from having recently watched the contrasting rock documentaries *Runnin' Down a Dream*, (about Tom Petty) directed by Peter Bogdanovich, and *Anvil: The Story of Anvil* directed by Sacha Gervasi. So what is this desire to be a rock star all about? I think it's a desire:

- ❖ To play loud and fast, on stage, in front of large (1,000 – 10,000) and appreciative audiences

- ❖ To make lots of money playing my own music

❖ For "no strings attached" intimacy (you know what I mean) with numerous women

❖ To travel

❖ For recognition from other artists I admire: Let's just say these are people I would like to have come up to me and say, "I like your music." Leo Kottke, The Smothers Brothers, Steve Martin, James Brown, Frank Zappa, John McLaughlin, Del Rey, Thelonious Monk, Marc Ribot, Chuck Berry, Nomeansno, Brian Eno, Robert Fripp, Bill Bruford, The Beatles, Nels Cline, Richard P. Feynman, Janet Feder, John Zorn, Tim Sparks, Mike Keneally, Henry Kaiser, John Fahey, Larry Coryell, David Grisman, The Bad Plus, Jello Biafra, Michael Hedges, Ani DiFranco, Steve Howe, Laurie Anderson, Paul Simon, Johnny Marr, Leonard Bernstein, Nick Hornby, Bill Drummond, Sting, Steven Soderberg, Pete Townshend, Garrison Kellior, Spaulding Gray...

No doubt theses desire are the remains of childhood dreams implanted by my hours of lip-synced, air guitar impersonations of Kiss, AC/DC, Judas Priest, and dozens of other heavy metal bands – and later, my genuine attempts at vocal and guitar imitations: But where do these desires leave me? Let me tackle them one by one.

Play loud and fast, on stage, in front of large and appreciative audiences

20 years ago, Boud Deun played loud and fast, on stage, but Boud Deun never played in front of more than 300-600 people. So this desire has never been fulfilled. I suspect some of this is ego, though goodness knows it would just be nice to play for more people. So how could I achieve this desire?

31

Hmm...hmmm... Aha! I have it! Shawn, if you want to play for bigger crowds, you should play rock and roll – not Modern Primitive Acoustic Scientist Music. And there it is:

My desire to be a "rock" star is misplaced. What I truly want is to play Modern Primitive Acoustic Scientist Music in front of large and appreciative audiences, and that almost never happens to anyone! Perhaps for a brief time in the early 1970s a few innovative progressive and fusion bands such as King Crimson and The Mahavishnu Orchestra (inspirations for my Modern Primitive style) managed to play for relatively large audiences but never since then. And most of the other artists I esteem from that time period – Captain Beefheart, The Hampton Grease Band, Univers Zero, John Fahey, et al. – rarely, if ever, played to sizeable audiences.

Then in the early 1980s, the punk bands I liked were not famous – sure they might get a few hundred people out to a gig but for the most part those bands were unequivocally underground. In fact I saw GWAR at The Hung Jury Pub in 1988 and there were only 12 people in the audience!

Where I really missed the boat was the early 1990s. There were many weird bands that were also popular – Primus, Sonic Youth...hmmm... Who else? I thought there were more avant-rock bands that had some mainstream success in the '90s. I might be able to include Mr. Bungle and/or Naked City but they never crossed over into the mainstream. So do two weird and popular bands from the 1990s count as many? Not at all! Goodness: Have I been deluding myself all these years? It appears so.

Make lots of money playing my own music

My friend, the offbeat blues-Americana singer and guitar and ukulele master Del Rey, has a line for musicians who complain about not making enough money: "You want to make money? Go get a job." I love that.

I say it to myself now, "You want to make more money? Go play rock and roll; or go apply for some grants." Both of which, in a sense, amount to having a job.

Casual (no strings attached) intimacy with numerous women

I'm afraid that I suffer from serial monogamy. Frankly, I can't complain.

Travel

Done. 36 countries visited thus far.

Recognition from other artists I admire

I look at the above list and I see a lot of people who are in fact my friends, acquaintances, or individuals with whom I've exchanged mutually respectful correspondence.

Hmmm...sometimes it's hard to find perspective, but not today.

I am a rock star!

16 May 2016, Monday

More refining of *Halloween* pieces: Specifically I worked on "Five Planets Visible With The Naked Eye" and "The Ninth..."

"Five..." is a wonderfully weird ersatz invention of sorts. It doesn't adhere to the rules of an invention, still, in my mind, it retains the spirit of one, so that's what I'm calling it. Today

I changed a few notes in the lower register part, trying to find a better balance of consonance and dissonance in relation to the higher register melody: There was nothing easy about this as the high-register melody is a perplexing but irresistible thread of unexpected intervals, chromaticism, and outrageously off kilter rhythmic figures.

Conversely, "The Ninth..." is a simple and pensive, pseudo-Asian sounding piece. I say "pseudo-Asian" because, as someone who has traveled extensively in Asia and studied the music of both China and Korea, to me "The Ninth..." is more akin to a Hollywood version of Asian music – there's nothing authentic about it. But that's okay because I wasn't trying to compose an Asian-sounding piece; I was just transcribing the music in my head. "The Ninth..." began to take on an Asian atmosphere when I started picking the nylon-string melody near the bridge, a technique I have been using for years because it adds tonal color and produces a sharp, infrequently heard guitar sound, comparable to that of a Chinese *guzheng* or Japanese *koto*.

18 May 2016, Wednesday

Today I gave a ninety-minute interview to Hank Hoffman for the *New Haven Arts Paper*. The paper asked Hank do a piece on an "edgy musician" – I'm flattered that he thought of me. A few of the usual questions were asked, and a few of my usual answers were given, but one fresh question about music education led to an epiphany: I want to be the Leonard Bernstein of rock and roll – a combination of artist, composer, performer, and educator. My History of Rock class is providing this opportunity. Ah, I haven't mentioned this yet...

I started teaching The History of Rock at the University of New Haven this past January. Gratefully I was able to create my own syllabus that, while venerating the pioneers of the

1950s and '60s such as, Sister Rosetta Tharpe, Bo Diddley, Chuck Berry, Berry Gordy and Motown, also features lesser-known innovators from later years, the Velvet Underground, Captain Beefheart, Devo, The Slits, Grand Master Flash, and Laurie Anderson, to name but a few. In short, while my rock and roll interests are broad, the focus of my curriculum is on weird and "outsider" rock. I suspect highlighting fringe artists will be true for my long-term rock and roll Bernstein-esque goals.

19 May 2016, Thursday

Spent a lot of time (one hour plus) practicing The Beatles song "Within You, Without You". What a stunning piece of music all around – George Harrison and George Martin at their best. It's a challenge to emulate the articulations of both the sitar and the Indian-string section – the slides and the bends I have to employ are different from those of rock or jazz guitarists – but the rewards are worth it.

20 May 2016, Friday

THE SCIENCE OF POPULAR MUSIC

Science fascinates me, but, lamentably, only on a superficial level. As soon as terminology gets complex or math is applied I get lost and become stultified: I possess no natural aptitude for any in-depth scientific understanding. Nevertheless, my reverence for science and scientists is immense.

Is a superficial familiarity with something enough to warrant admiration? It certainly is for me. A scientist (or anyone else) without a deep understanding of rhythm, melody, harmony, etc., can still love music. So why can't the same be true for a musician regarding science?

Ah, but I contradict myself. I have found that a superficial familiarity with music will all too frequently result in misplaced reverence, particularly concerning popular music [see 17 September 2016 "*Pet Sounds* and the Misattribution of Value"]. Do scientists look at someone like me – whose understanding of science is limited to popular references – and sarcastically think, "Oh you like Brian Cox's *The Infinite Monkey Cage*, do you? And you read Michio Kaku's *Physics of the Future*? And you've watched both Neil deGrasse Tyson's *and* Carl Sagan's *Cosmos*? Humph. You should listen to someone who actually knows what he's talking about, *real* science would make your cerebral cortex explode!" I doubt scientists think that way. For all their popularity and mainstream recognition Cox, Kaku, Tyson, and Sagan are all well-educated and highly respected scientists.

But this train of thought does suggest a big difference between science and popular music: In science, new theories and practices are studiously developed through years of hard work and an understanding of what has come before; popular music does the opposite.

21 May 2016, Saturday

Played a fabulous gig tonight with the '80s band. Two solid sets, an enthusiastic crowd, and no soundman (soundmen are the second worst people to deal with at a show; musicians are the worst), so we controlled the overall volume from the stage. This made a huge difference in my enjoyment of the evening. Note to all soundmen and bands, "Turn down!" No band in a club ever needs to be louder than The Beatles were in The Cavern.

22 May 2016, Sunday

I presented a fun and satisfying EarthQuaker Devices clinic at Sam Ash today; well-attended with encouraging feedback.

One attendee tweeted, "...loved every second of Shawn's demo, he knows pedals and he's a great player!" That's flattering, because it was my first pedal clinic in more than a year, so I felt I was just getting into the swing of things...

This is a major issue with many of my public performances, they are too infrequent for me to get into a seamless routine. When I was touring in the early 2000s, my shtick was superb. I could play the same songs and tell the same jokes three nights in a row, in three different cities, and perfect them. I miss that. A second pedal clinic is scheduled two weeks from now, and while that offers me time to work on the presentation at home, prepping is not as advantageous as performing in front of an audience.

24 May 2016, Tuesday

Stirred by further practice of "Within You, Without You", this morning I added more articulation nuances – grace notes, slides, and bends – to "The Ninth..." A few days ago I wrote about the unintentional Asian influence prevalent in this piece, now there is an overt Indian influence as well!

26 May 2016, Thursday

Spent the morning filming and editing a video lesson for my website www.WeirdGuitarLessons.com on the psychedelic instrumental section of The Beatles' "Being For The Benefit Of Mr. Kite". The idea came to me at a recent *Sgt. Pepper's* rehearsal when I impulsively stepped on my Arpanoid pedal and out flew a swarm of swirling and modulating notes that were perfect for the part. The lesson is alarmingly unflashy if you're into guitar virtuosity, but downright perfect if you're a Beatles fan or fond of "noise" as music.

27 May 2016, Friday

Currently reading Ralph Kirkpatrick's *Interpreting Bach's Well-Tempered Clavier* and Dan LeRoy's *The Beastie Boys' Paul's Boutique (33 1/3)*. How are those two disparate titles for juxtaposition? Credibly, the fundamental precept to be garnered from reading these two books side-by-side is that Kirkpatrick is overly pedantic:

> In measure 1, the first suspension in the alto on B, and to a certain extent its preparation on F-sharp, can be brought out by using the dissonant passing note on C-sharp in the bass. E, the fourth bass note in this measure, is a perfectly bland consonance unless one chooses to hear it in relation to the alto F-sharp.
> [p. 100]

And LeRoy is too anecdotal:

> …the idea that it might be fun to throw eggs at these people…the $11,000 rent the band paid each month still beat the cost of three $200-a-night hotel rooms…They went to the Record Plant. And the first thing they did was, Mike D called a barroom rental place, and he got a large-screen projection television, a Ping-Pong table, a foosball table… [pp. 33, 39, 48]

There is a midway point that can be found between these two approaches (both of which do have their merits, regardless of my criticism), Robert Greenberg's lectures for The Great Courses (*How to Listen to and Understand Great Music, Bach and the High Baroque*, etc.) and Walter Everett's *The Beatles as Musicians* both typify this balance of agreeable academic theory and useful trivia.

29 May 2016, Sunday

The Luck Pushers had a pleasurable gig last night at a country club, however it was definitely "work". We unexpectedly got moved outside, which was dark – this made it tricky to see the fretboard – and infiltrated by rapacious mosquitoes. I also broke a string at the beginning of the second set and found it impossible to replace it in the shadows of the half moon, so I abandoned the endeavor and played a dozen songs without a B string. I managed passably well (I pulled off a half-good solo on a funky, Aretha Franklin-esque version of "The Weight") but I wouldn't recommend it. Instead, always pack a second guitar and a flashlight.

30 May 2016, Monday

Finished reading Kirkpatrick's *Interpreting Bach's WTC*, which has a magnanimous preface and introduction, "…my hope is to enlighten rather than to prove a point." Followed by one hundred plus pages of punctilious instruction (possibly injunctions). Finally, the book comes to a close on the penultimate page with a most contemplative, if ironic – considering the previous hundred plus pages –, statement:

> Overstatement of details [in regard to performance] can sometimes produce understatement of a work as a whole. Yet how often can significant understatement add up to overwhelming eloquence! [p. 128]

My humble assessment aside, I'm glad to have read it. The final six pages of the book coalesced Kirkpatrick's opinions and perspectives on performance in a succinct and pleasing manner. His overzealous point-of-view may be a useful reference when recording *Halloween*: There is much to be said for being fanatically punctilious (though not overly precious) when it comes to creating your art. As I plan to record and mix *Halloween* completely on my own, in my home studio (this is not the greatest of ideas but it's practical), I think it would be prudent to have some encouraging and sensible words of wisdom ringing in my ears.

JUNE

1 June 2016, Wednesday

CULTIVATING INSOUCIANCE

With no false modesty (and with a modicum of chagrin) I must admit there are a number of serious faults and limitations with my solo fingerstyle guitar technique. This is due in part to: 1) my lack of regular practice (and performance opportunities), 2) my lack of desire to perfect my technique, and 3) my self-limiting belief that it's "good enough." Let's address these one at a time.

1) My lack of regular practice and performance opportunities stems from two issues: I like to play many different styles of guitar, so fingerstyle is only one of many techniques that require my attention. Furthermore, I more or less stopped performing solo fingerstyle guitar in 2005. At that point, I

believed I had created music that was unique in the world of fingerstyle guitar, i.e. *The Art of Modern Primitive Guitar* – an album that offers distinctive melodic and rhythmic material more akin to 20th century classical music than to the "fingerstyle" genre, but it is *not* classical music. Lamentably the majority of guitarists and guitar-music fans seemed uninterested in my Modern Primitive Guitar style (though the record was a critical success). I'm embarrassed to admit that the album's lackluster commercial success psychologically stalled my fingerstyle career before I literally stalled it.

2) My lack of desire to perfect my technique arises from the indictment that…it's just too darn hard and it takes too much time. Regardless of those feeble excuses, I could never get the music perfect anyway – not like I hear it in my head. Besides that, most of my favorite musicians are sloppy players. I join their ranks gladly! (These are all wretched justifications; I should practice more.)

3) My self-limiting belief that it's "good enough" is not actually true; my playing could and should be better. But I am habitually disposed to practice only as much as I need to, to get the point across. Years later I felt vindicated (rightly or wrongly) for accommodating this pitiable attitude when I read Salvador Dali's words in *Diary of a Genius* regarding his early surrealist works:

> Of course I would not hear anything about technique while I was busy creating the Dalinian cosmogony, with its limp watches, which prophesied the disintegration of matter…I did not even have time to paint it all as it should have been. It was good enough if my meaning was clear. [p. 22]

Goodness, those words sounded like my excuses! (They also clarified something important: I always thought Dali's early paintings, such as *Inaugural Gooseflesh* [1928] and *The Persistence*

43

of Memory [1931], were beguiling ideas yet were not fully realized, especially in comparison to his later works like *Raphaelesque Head Exploding* [1951] or *The Sacrament of the Last Supper* [1955]: Dali agreed!)

But here's the rub: Dali went on to write, "The next generation would see to it that my work was finished and refined." [p. 22] Meaning, either the next generation of artists would be encouraged to take Dali's innovations and technique to the next level, or, as I've always interpreted that sentence, as he himself got older, he would become more diligent and thorough (which he did). Perhaps I should as well.

My last word on this topic of technique: In 2012 John Stropes – guitarist, educator, and founder of the first university degree program for fingerstyle guitar – invited me to the University of Milwaukee, Peck School of the Arts, to examine their music library for research on my book *The 50 Greatest Guitar Books*. Stropes also suggested that I should present a guitar masterclass to his students. Now by that time I had forsaken my fingerstyle playing for roughly seven years and had I known beforehand the ridiculously high caliber of technical ability his students possessed I'm not sure I would have said yes.

I presented my masterclass and found it rewarding in regard to content – primarily my personal approach to composition, which I noted was more akin to The Minutemen and Anton Webern than to Chet Atkins –, if sloppy and under-rehearsed in performance.

Luckily it was only after my lecture that I heard Stropes' students play; their technique far surpassed my own. And their skills included a superfluity of qualities – tone, speed, agility, dynamics, and endurance. It was eye opening. I always knew my facility was below what my potential offered, but these kids outshined me on my best day...when it comes to technique that is. But for me...

"For me, the art was before, later the technique." - Alejandro Jodorowsky, from *Jodorowsky's Dune*

2 June 2016, Thursday

Progress was made on *Halloween* today as I modally transposed "Eleven Days Disappeared" into a minor key, which gave it new life. "Eleven..." hasn't been the easiest of pieces to arrange, so I've been experimenting with an assortment of rhythmic and harmonic variations: This minor key modification is the first one I've been happy with since the piece's inception.

I also rehearsed some Jackson Browne material, as I recently started playing with a tribute band called Running On Empty (R.O.E.). Technically speaking, Browne's music is pretty straightforward, but I'm finding it challenging to memorize some of his chord progressions because several of them are similar, and many of these songs are brand new to me (I know Browne's hits but not his deep-cuts).

3 June 2016, Friday

Today, while reading *A Year With Swollen Appendices: Brian Eno's Diary*, I learned of Michael Nyman's piece "1-100" (1976). "1-100" is built around the musical concept and implications of *decay*. My 8-string baritone "Etude No. 1" is also, partially, based on this idea. I had not considered the decay aspect of my etude as anything original or innovative but I didn't know of any other works, from other composers, that had employed the concept so expressly. Now I do! Thanks, Nyman. Thanks, Eno. I'm listening to it right now online. It's lovely.

PRESTER JOHN AND THE BMAD

Last night I attended a screening of a documentary at The New Haven Film Festival in which I was featured as a talking head. The film was about the BMAD, which stands for Bethany Music and Dance, and which is…hmmm…how best to describe the BMAD?

One Friday each month, Bill Fischer, the man who initiated and maintains the BMAD, opens his house to anyone – seriously, *anyone* can come – to play music, listen to music, and dance to music in his "ballroom", which is in fact an old barn. Bill has been hosting these BMAD events once a month for 25 years! I've attended BMAD parties that had more than 200 people in attendance, and while Bill's house might be square-footage big, most of the rooms are more cozy than capacious – if you come to the BMAD you better like people and be comfortable with a meager amount of personal space. Bill's house is divided up into several rooms, all of which become genre-specific music rooms during the BMAD: the old-time room, the bluegrass room, the swing room, the sing-along room, the aforementioned converted barn for dancing, and the catchall room. Every now and then you'll hear a Beatles or John Denver song in the catchall room, otherwise the music played at the BMAD tends to be folk based. The music is also primarily acoustic, played on guitars, banjos, fiddles, mandolins, penny whistles, etc. The dance features contra dancing accompanied by a variety of old-time, bluegrass, and Irish folk songs. The dance music is provided by any number of musicians not preoccupied in the other rooms.

Those are the basic facts. But what are the feelings the BMAD arouses? Joy, hope, camaraderie, pleasure, trust, and love. Simply put, BMAD parties are some of the most wonderful experiences I have ever had. And there is one specific story regarding the power of the BMAD that just happens to be about my first visit.

It was October of 2007. I arrived early – I might have been too early, I was the first person there, but Bill didn't seem to mind – so I got to see everyone, dozens and dozens of people, trickle in. Eventually I settled in with a group of musicians – another guitarist, fiddler, banjo player, and mandolinist – jamming in the catchall room.

We played a couple of Irish and old-time standards, "Red Haired Boy" and "Over the Waterfall", and then someone proposed we play "June Apple". Now I had learned "June Apple" years earlier from *Doc Watson in Nashville: Good Deal!* but I rarely got to play it with anyone, so I was delighted by the suggestion. At a breakneck speed, we all took turns playing the melody, with each musician good-naturedly trying to outdo the other with his or her own individual interpretation, but when the mandolinist stepped forward for his chance the game changed completely. His fingers blurred across the fretboard playing spry and sophisticated variations on the melody.

We finished "June Apple" and, thrilled by the mandolinist's skill and refined melodic sensibility, I asked, "Do you play any David Grisman?"

"Of course," he responded coolly and jumped into Grisman's version of "Minor Swing" (composed by Django Reinhardt and Stéphane Grappelli, though Grisman's version is notably different). As he had done on the previous tune, the mandolinist performed a stellar, classically influenced solo. I was awestruck. As a result, my train of thought went like this: Irish folk music, Doc Watson, David Grisman, Django Reinhardt, Stéphane Grappelli…

"Do you play any Frank Zappa?" I asked.

"Sure." he said and nonchalantly launched into Zappa's "Peaches en Regalia". I was ecstatic! I couldn't believe it! My first time at the BMAD (and as it turned out, the mandolinist's first time too) and I'd found a musical soulmate! That was David Miller, my soon-to-be partner in Prester John, and I can say without a doubt, one of the finest musicians I have ever played with and perhaps the smartest and most humble man I have ever met.

That story might seem to be about me and David Miller and Prester John, but it's actually about the power of the BMAD and the musical and patrimonial contributions Bill Fischer has made to his community.

Because of such contributions, the Italian filmmaker Anna Marra has made a film documenting such events. Besides filming BMAD jams and dances, Anna also interviewed several regular attendees who served as talking heads throughout the film. Bill suggested she interview me: Hence my presence in the movie, all of 45 seconds of it (cut down from 45 minutes of filmed interview). I was honored.

6 June 2016, Monday

One thematic concept I'm working with in *Halloween* is to highlight the musical interval that corresponds with each title. For instance, the distance between the opening notes of the 6-string and the nylon in "Six..." is a sixth. Similarly, in "The Ninth..." the distance between the baritone root note and the nylon's opening melodic note is a ninth. And the first two notes of "One..." are the same – a unison – and that interval has, in mathematical terms, a 1:1 ratio. I haven't been dogmatic about this – some pieces just want to do what they want to do. Still, the pieces that don't feature this intervallic concept do contain some other sort of musical/ numerical/

title connection. Unfortunately I can't take credit for this idea; I appropriated (stole) it from J.S. Bach. Bach featured the same "intervals as theme" concept in the canons included in his *Goldberg Variations*.

7 June 2016, Tuesday

Started reading *The Art of Practicing* by Madeline Bruser, which motivated me to set up a stereo in my kids' room. Bruser writes of several of her students' earliest recollections of musical inspiration; students who at a young age were so moved by a specific musical event that at that very moment they aspired to become musicians themselves. This called to mind my own such memories that include a cheap, portable, fatigue-green record player with a built-in speaker that, at the age of five, I played ceaselessly. Thus I installed a stereo in my kids' room with the undisguised hope of turning them into, if not musicians than at least life-long music fans. No, that's not true: I want them to be musicians – and I want to play bass in their band.

SHAWN BUYS A KISS RECORD

When I was six-years-old, I told my mom that I had heard a song on the radio and that I'd like to buy the record...but, I didn't know what the song was called or who played it. Undaunted, my mom took me to a record store in downtown Slidell, Louisiana, and told the tall, wiry teenage clerk that I wanted to buy this unknown record.

"Well...what does it sound like?" He asked, genuinely curious and wanting to be helpful.

Unfortunately, I could only respond with a self-conscious shrug of my shoulders.

The clerk nodded knowingly. He then turned and flipped through the row of 45s behind the counter, grabbed a single with a tan label, put it on the turntable, and cranked it up. "Is that it?" He yelled over Kiss' "Shout It Out Loud".

I shook my head with an affirmative waggle, looking back and forth between the clerk and my mom, and grinning ear to earsplitting ear. "We'll take it," my Mom shouted with a thumbs-up.

The memory of my shy, wordless exchange between the clerk and my mom leads me to believe that the record I had heard on the radio was most likely *not* "Shout It Out Loud", but that hardly mattered: The autumn of 1977 was swarming with first-graders buying Kiss records, so why not me?

This transformative event, and the joyous, primal feeling I was struck by when those stereo speakers started moving Kiss air, was life-changing. It is no hyperbole to say that this was the pivotal moment when I suddenly became aware that I wanted to be a musician. Specifically, I wanted to be Gene Simmons.

Postscript

For Christmas 1977 my parents (aka Santa) gave me a yellow, pressboard, child-sized acoustic guitar with a colorful, macramé-esque decal surrounding the soundhole. Rather than being grateful, I was annoyed. "That's not what Gene Simmons plays!" I told my parents. And I never played a note on that guitar (although my Mom still has it).

I didn't get or play another guitar until my fourteenth birthday. That one, which was also from my parents, I played a lot!

8 June 2016, Wednesday

Today I composed a fifth etude for the "8" that was inspired by Leo Brouwer's "Etude No. 4" from *20 Estudios Sencillos*. I even gave it a subtitle, "Chinese Astronomy". Now I know almost nothing about Chinese astronomy, or astronomy period, but I love the names given to the four regions of the sky by early Chinese astronomers: Azure Dragon, Black Tortoise, White Tiger, and Vermilion Bird, collectively known as the Four Symbols. As my new etude is composed of one four-measure phrase that is then repeated a second time with a slight variation, a third time almost identical to the first but with dynamic changes, and a fourth time almost identical to the second, these four groups of four brought to mind the Four Symbols. I realize this connection is tenuous at best but that's one of the beauties of artistic license!

However, as the etude itself is dark (harmonically speaking it's in the Phrygian mode) yet rhythmically very sprightly, I could use ad hoc reasoning to claim that each four-measure phrase also represents the movement of each of the Four Symbol animals…hmmm…this wasn't true…but now that I've thought of it, perhaps I can play with this idea. This should be fun! I'm off to play dragon, tortoise, tiger, and bird!

9 June 2016, Thursday

Presented a unique EarthQuaker Devices demo at the Sam Ash in Paramus, NJ tonight. Customarily I perform a bit of a shtick while demoing these pedals – but tonight was an unprecedented, hour-long Q&A session with a gregarious and witty audience; very gratifying.

18 June 2016, Saturday

Today was long and weird (but not the good kind).

During the dress rehearsal for the *Sgt. Pepper's Lonely Hearts Club Band* performance I entered into a huge public argument (huge by my standards; I'm not a confrontational person); an embarrassing shouting match, with curses (mine) regarding the proper placement of the tambourine on "While My Guitar Gently Weeps". I was adamant that it should be played as on the record, particularly during the two **B** section verses after the guitar solo, which finds the tambourine on beat 4 for the first eight measures and beat 2 for the next eight. Now that might seem like nitpicking, yet this part is remarkable in that it tone paints the lyrics, "you were *inverted* too", with "too" also serving as a brilliant pun. The person I was arguing with didn't think this mattered at all and I found this immensely frustrating, especially considering that the percussionist should have already known the part, and, even though he didn't, with a brief note it would have been easy to perform. In many ways this argument, for me, cast a shadow over the entire evening.

The concert itself was fine, if anti-climatic since it was a one-off performance. It required a lot of effort from everyone involved (more than a dozen musicians) and one performance is not enough to do this music justice. I was rather depressed on the ride home but I reminded myself, "This too shall pass," and I leaned into the sadness rather than denying it.

22 June 2016, Wednesday

Oh how I would love to reconcile (or at least be able to codify) my feelings regarding art vs. commerce. While watching *I'm Not There*, Todd Haynes' film about Bob Dylan, I began wondering if my idealistic, Dylan-esque, hippie/punk principles regarding culture and commercialism are relevant anymore. Such as my belief that iconic songs of the past 50 years should not be used to sell cars or fast food, or serve any other such crass purpose: Art for Art's sake (which may generate commerce, but that is not its goal), and products for consumerism.

But perhaps I need to reframe my thoughts on consumerism. For instance, the dilemma that occurs when a commercial – the content of which is out of my control – pops up on

YouTube before one of my own songs or instructional videos. What am I to think? Truthfully, the first thing I think is, "I wonder how many commercials need to play before I get paid? Because up to now I have not been paid at all."

And look at that, the first thing that came to mind was "Where is my money?" Not "Is it art?" or "Maybe I should demonetize my videos." or "That was tasteful/ tasteless/ discreet/ crass/ inspiring/ demoralizing/ etc." I'm hoping that admitting my own avaricious feelings is a start towards codification and reconciliation because I'm unable to either embrace or justify these contradictions.

Later: I wrote the above entry at 7:45am. At 8:20am I picked up Stephen Nachmanovitch's *Free Play* and read:

> Reasoned knowledge proceeds from information of which we're consciously aware–only a partial sampling of our total knowledge. Intuitive knowledge, on the other hand, proceeds from everything we know and everything we are. It converges on the moment from a rich plurality of directions and sources–hence the feeling of absolute certainty that is traditionally associated with intuitive knowledge.
> [p. 40]

From that I take: "Shawn, yours is not to wonder why but to do – trust your instincts, let the rest sort itself out. Why should you concern yourself with art vs. commerce? Just do the work that *wants* to be done." And so I do. I never create my art to make a buck. If I did, I certainly wouldn't be very smart composing etudes for an 8-string baritone guitar that almost no one owns!

23 June 2016, Thursday

ON RELATIVE FAME, RECOGNITION, INFLUENCE, AND INSPIRATION

Yesterday the guitarist Glenn Phillips "friended" me on Facebook and messaged, "Good to hear from you, Shawn – here's hoping we cross paths in person sometime soon." If I dwell upon this, it delights me more than I can properly explain – but I'll try:

Most people have no idea who Glenn Phillips is or that he helped create one of the most exceptional albums ever made – an album most people have never even heard of –, the 1971 release *Music to Eat* by The Hampton Grease Band. *Music to Eat* is laudable for several reasons:

❖ It's a debut double album: Only Frank Zappa and Chicago did that prior to *Music to Eat*.

❖ There are only seven songs on that double album!

❖ It's been said (most likely apocryphally but it's good legend) that *Music to Eat* is the second-lowest selling album in the history of Columbia records.

❖ It's a masterpiece!

Identifying *Music to Eat* as parts Frank Zappa and Captain Beefheart isn't a stretch, the influence of both those artists is obvious, but one can also reference disparate elements culled from The Allman Brothers Band, John Coltrane (the guitar solos are at times *A Love Supreme*-esque), and Flamenco music, and cite lyrics pilfered from a spray paint can! But the most striking thing about *Music to Eat* is how it presages punk and new wave bands of the 1970s and early '80s, particularly

Richard Hell, Pere Ubu, and the Minutemen. In short, *Music to Eat* is so far ahead of its time that, except for the technologically lo-fi recording, it's ahead of *our* time.

I was lucky enough to come across a copy of *Music to Eat* when I was 18 years old and working at a used record store…

I can't do it. I can't properly celebrate, let alone summarize, this album in words. It's too good and nothing I could write would do it justice. You'll have to listen for yourself. You can find it online. Start with the opening track "Halifax" and do not turn it off before the 13-minute mark (the song tracks in at just under 20 minutes). If you do listen beyond 13 minutes, you'll listen forever…

So, yesterday, there is Glenn Phillips, a huge influence on my guitar playing* communicating with me on Facebook – and no one will ever care but me (and maybe him). It's moments like that that put fame, recognition, influence, and inspiration into perspective – even if the perspective is blurry.

24 June 2016, Friday

Revisited the impishly adroit 8-string baritone "Etude No. 4" today. I began composing this piece in December 2013, worked on it briefly in January 2014, but left it unfinished until now. It is close to completion but will require careful attention. The **B** section is currently a waltz that is too reminiscent of the **D** section of "Etude No. 3". I think I could make it more charismatic by cajoling it out of 3/4 and convincing it to become a puckish, stop-time dance in 2/4.

---

* During my year studying at Musicians Institute I spent a large portion of my time learning guitar licks from *Music to Eat* (played by Phillips and Harold Kelling). I went so far as to rip off one lick from a solo in "Halifax" (I don't know if it's Phillips or Kelling) for use in the solo section of my song "Domesticated".

I also played with the Four Symbols, animal movement, concept I thought up for "Etude No. 5". I'm afraid I might be forcing this idea. "Chinese Astronomy" wants to do what it wants to do, and the phrasing is more effective if I approach it like a Shakespearean actor – pausing, hesitating, rushing, even stumbling (intentionally) over his or her lines. I love the animal movement idea, so perhaps I'll use it in another piece, but it's not working for "Chinese Astronomy".

26 June 2016, Sunday

I had a delightful conversation with Del Rey today. She is such a refreshing person (and an extraordinary guitar player) and possesses an auspicious equilibrium of alacrity and misanthropy. She and I have much in common, excluding our parental role models: She affectionately describes her father as a "ne'er–do–well", whereas I would describe both my parents as dark horse champions. I also envy Del's inherent devil-may-care attitude as compared to my innate yearning to be liked – my McCartney to her Lennon. (Many who know me well or who have seen me in my most contemptuous moments might think, "Your yearning to be liked? You're not trying very hard." The truth is, as derisive as I can be sometimes, I could be much worse.)

Musically it might appear that Del and I have little in common. Del's style is steeped in the genres of Americana and blues. I tend to avoid any association with those traditions, not because I dislike them but because they're not me – I have no connection with roots music beyond listening pleasure*. Still, Del maintains a fringe approach to the blues,

---

* If I were to make an argument for a personal connection to roots music – in particular old-time, bluegrass, and country music – it would be via my West Virginia hillbilly heritage: I'm only one generation removed from living in a clapboard shack with no electricity, a hand-pumped well for drinking water, and an outhouse for when nature calls.

such as performing, on the guitar and uke, a vast amount of intricate, polyphonic material culled from the boogie-woogie piano canon with sophisticated "uptown" chord substitutions. She has also arranged some very hip and complex tunes by Noel Coward, Trinidadian calypso musician George Browne (aka Young Tiger), and Theodor Geisel (better known as Dr. Seuss).

As a result of her inimitable approach, Del has faced some of the same issues I have regarding the difficulty of building and maintain an audience: Trying to attract listeners who are willing to embrace a wide range of musical content as well as tolerate idiosyncratic material ostensibly outside of what an idiomatic genre is supposed to conform to. Thus, Del and I get along swimmingly.

My conversation with Del provided some fresh perspective and practical advice on art vs. commerce. For example, regarding the significance of this book's subtitle options, *A Year In The Life Of An Unknown Artist* vs. *Musician* vs. *Guitarist*, Del pointed out that this is a commercial concern. If I think "Guitarist" would sell more books even though "Artist" has more personal legitimacy, it's obvious that I should choose "Artist" because "Guitarist" is the sell-out. Yet "Musician" is more expansive than "Guitarist" and less vague than "Artist": "Musician", without compromise, is dignified and latitudinous. Thank you Del.

27 June 2016, Monday

A productive, four-hour R.O.E. rehearsal last night: It is possible I played more slide guitar yesterday than I ever have in my life. I could come to enjoy that – except that slide requires a big commitment in order to finesse the intonation and maintain a rich, full tone. Speaking strictly of the Jackson Browne songs, I haven't mentally or physically absorbed the original recordings' solos, but I'm unwilling to practice slide at home if I'm not going to play it regularly. And why am I not playing slide in this band? Because legendary guitarist Arlen Roth is! And rightfully so. However, Arlen wasn't there last night, so I filled in.

28 June 2016, Tuesday

Paraphrasing Brian Eno (from "Unthinkable Futures"): "Check the originality and scope of your ideas." Sound advice in the planning stages of most creative activities: Accordingly, I have been listening to a fair amount of string quartet music, from Beethoven's 16 revolutionary quartets to Kronos Quartet commissioned works. I've also been investigating guitar quartet music, most of which is predictably guitaristic – lots of strumming, arpeggios, and solos – and which I have little or no interest in. As I've mentioned, *Halloween* was originally composed and arranged for musical registers rather than specific instrumentation, hence the music is lacking the usual guitar articulations (there is only one fully-articulated chord in the entirety of *Halloween*). Consequently, *Halloween* has more in common with a string or woodwind quartet than with a guitar ensemble. I like this. Not only does this set *Halloween* apart from other guitar quartets, it also makes it possible for a string, woodwind, or any other quartet – or small chamber group duplicating parts – to perform the work.

29 June 2016, Wednesday

I'm on a train to Boston to catch a plane to China! A trip to China is, of course, exciting in itself, yet the instinctive exhilaration I'm feeling stems largely from the act of traveling itself – the movement.

In 1999 I decided to leave my life in Virginia behind and do the Grand Tour of Europe – with a few sojourns to North Africa. Before I left on my trip, one of my students gave me a pocket-sized book called *The Quotable Traveler* with quotes gathered from the works of diverse writers such as Samuel Johnson – "The use of traveling is to regulate imagination and reality, and instead of thinking how things may be, to see them as they are." – and Douglas Adams – "Don't Panic!" It was a charming book and a thoughtful gift. As I flipped through it I noticed I had "read that, read that, read that, read that twice, read that..." Clearly I was meant to "Keep moving." – Hunter S. Thompson.*

• • •

Boston: A pleasant evening with Wang Ao, my host for this trip to China. Wang, a guitar student of mine, is a Chinese poet and scholar who teaches at Wesleyan University. He has invited me on this trip to observe his presentation on the lyrics and music of John Lennon, a presentation I helped him create.

---

* When I was 14 years old, all 10th grade English classes at my school were assigned to write a letter to a famous, living, American author. Only two students got a response, I was one of them. My letter was to Hunter S. Thompson. He wrote his answers in the margins of my original letter: "Yes," "Never", "Ho, ho", "Money", and "Good luck with yr. bullshit + stay away from whiskey."

JULY

1 July 2016, Friday

It's 3am Saturday morning in Shenzhen, China (3pm Friday afternoon back home). 32 hours of exhausting travel. Finally, we're at the hotel.

• • •

2 July 2016, Saturday

Walked around the hotel's neighborhood for an hour. Oh the smell, I love this smell: The pungent aroma of cheap, but authentically Chinese ramen noodle soups, hot peppers, and roast duck, mixed with the heat and humidity of southern China's natural environment. It's a peculiar but pleasant combination of spicy, sour, piquant, and damp.

• • •

Spent most of the evening at Enclave, the bookstore Wang will be lecturing at tomorrow night. The location is quintessential China in transition. The district is a juxtaposition of vacant, run down 1970s factories and new, high-end shops selling luxury items, waiting for the future to catch up (it will, in less than six months I imagine). The building in which the bookstore is located is a muddled permutation of old and new. The ground floor is effectively demolished except for the structural skeleton (support columns but no walls); the entrance ramp to the elevator is "guarded" by several stray dogs and festooned with dirt, sand, and dripping water; and the elevator looks as though it was built with scrap material found in a five-and-dime remainder bin (ironically it is the smoothest elevator I've ever ridden in). But when you get off at the fifth floor, voilà, you are transported to what appears to be an American, undoubtedly hip, and shamelessly fussy, boutique poetry bookstore. Then you notice all the books are in Chinese – even the English ones. They are elegantly stacked on rustic wooden shelves, against attractive exposed brick, under stylish industrial piping. China or Seattle? Walk outside, you won't ask again.

3 July 2016, Sunday

Flipping through TV channels at 4am I came across a program titled "Girls Fighting": Essentially an American reality TV show cum China, with a cut-to-the-chase title.

How astounding it is to be 8,000 miles away from home and have so many things be the same. As I write this I'm thinking, "How sad it is to be 8,000 miles away from home and have so many things be the same." Hmmm...yes...I could write on this extensively but I'm not sure that I want to open that can of worms, could do it justice, and wouldn't end up resembling a cynical old man. Still...

Shenzhen is more akin to San Diego, CA, than to the ancient gray brick-and-terracotta-tiled China of my childhood dreams – a China that was still in existence during my first visit in 2000 but has been slowly disappearing since. Or has been preserved in the most contrived of ways, as tourist attractions, equivalent to Williamsburg, VA, or Old Sturbridge Village, MA.

For instance, in 2000 I visited a charming little village called Dali, which encapsulated what I thought the architecture of China should look like – latticework ceilings and walls, interlocking wooden beams painted a distinctive red and green, and roofs with sweeping curves rising at the corners. It was a perfect realization of my American vision of China, induced by Szechuan Delight restaurant menus and the badly dubbed kung fu movies of my childhood.

When I returned to Dali in 2007 I was shocked to find that all the old buildings had been torn down only to be replaced with exact replicas! I hate to sound like a Luddite but I was appalled to find that all the charm that Dali had possessed in 2000 had been stripped away by "improvements". In all fairness the Dali buildings in 2000 did look like they were on the verge of collapsing (the improvements were probably structurally important), nevertheless, I was heartbroken. Dali had lost all its authenticity, reduced to a backlot of a movie studio. The irony of my effrontery was made apparent when I went on to visit Lijiang, a city I had not visited in 2000. I redemptively found Lijiang even more authentically Chinese than Dali had been in 2000; only to realize later that Lijiang was also a replica! That was a defining moment in my life regarding perspective and reality.

4 July 2016, Monday

TALKING ABOUT MUSIC IN CHINA

Last night Wang presented his "Lennon's DNA" lecture at Enclave. Before he began, Wang introduced me as his guest and "Beatles expert", magnanimously acknowledging that I had helped him prepare the talk. In the lecture Wang first analyzed Lennon's lyrics – citing the influence of Edward Lear and Lewis Carroll on Lennon's word play and imagery – and then demonstrated how his chord progressions – most notably his all-major-chord-progressions-that-don't-conform-to-any-one-key, as in "I Am The Walrus" – and melodies tone paint the lyrics.

After the presentation, a 20-something, Chinese college kid came up to me and stated emphatically, "I play guitar. I like heavy metal. That is rock and roll to me. I don't think The Beatles are rock and roll. Why do you say The Beatles are rock and roll?"

Rather than being willfully contrary, I could tell he was looking for a legitimate answer, so I asked, "What metal bands do you like?"

"Metallica," he tersely replied.

"Perfect. I like Metallica too. I also like Slayer and Anthrax and many other metal bands. But one thing that distinguishes Metallica is their sense of melody. I..."

Nodding his head in the affirmative the young man interrupted, "Yes, yes, exactly. I agree exactly, melody."

"Great," I said. "And where does Metallica get their sense of melody? From Black Sabbath. Other metal bands from the 1970s too, but for my money Black Sabbath are not only the fathers of heavy metal, they are also the most consistently strong songwriters of that period and effortlessly incorporated catchy melodic content into extremely heavy music. *And* they were a huge influence on Metallica – not to mention every other metal band."

The young man kept nodding his head in agreement.

"Where do you think Black Sabbath got their sense of melody from?" I paused for effect. "The Beatles. Ozzy Osbourne has said many times that hearing 'She Loves You' was like being hit by a bolt of lighting, that it changed his life. So look how short the trip is from Metallica to The Beatles, it's only one stop, Black Sabbath. Now Ozzy's personal testimony doesn't have to convince you but hopefully it's a good start."

"If you do start your own investigation into more Beatles music I suggest skipping 'She Loves You', as you probably won't call that 'rock and roll' because it certainly isn't Metallica. But check out 'Helter Skelter', 'Revolution', and

'She's So Heavy'. And 'Hey Bulldog'. Do you know what 'chromatic' means? A chromatic riff?"

"Yes. I am applying to the Berklee School of Music next year. I know what a chromatic riff is."

"Excellent. Well the riff in The Beatles' 'Hey Bulldog' is textbook Metallica, full of sinister chromaticism!"

The young man smiled shrewdly and suggested, "You talk about Metallica like I think about Metallica..." He kept nodding and I could tell he was contemplating, "Maybe The Beatles are rock and roll."

Later, while speaking with another group of students, the topic of singing came up. I suggested that everyone should sing, as it's natural and life affirming. A teenage girl interjected, "I would like to sing but I don't think I have a pretty voice." I responded with, "Maybe you don't. Maybe you have an ugly voice. But do you only watch pretty movies? Or read pretty books? Or look at pretty art? Music doesn't always have to be pretty. Find out what your voice *can* do and *do* that with your voice." Suddenly she got a gleam in her eye and announced eagerly, "Yes! Maybe I could be the world's ugliest singer!" "Maybe you could," I replied, "Just don't let it go to your head."

Postscript: These stories are particularly poignant to me because only hours earlier Wang and I were discussing music education in general, and specifically in reference to China. Wang claimed, "No one in China really knows about rock and roll history. They think rock and roll is loud, fast guitar playing, and long hair. The Beatles are not rock and roll to Chinese people. My friends in Beijing ask, 'Why are you doing a class on The Beatles? They are not rock and roll.' We [meaning Wang and myself] need to change the way rock and roll is appreciated in China."

Last night was the first step towards that new appreciation.

••••

I should mention that Wang, and poetry in general, are quite popular and well respected in China. Consequently, last night, in addition to presenting his lecture, Wang spent a good part of the evening signing copies of his recently published translation of Seamus Heaney poems.

5 July 2016, Tuesday

Shenzhen to Beijing, Beijing to Zurich, Zurich to Boston, Boston to New Haven. I need a better travel agent!

6 July 2016, Wednesday

59 years ago today John Lennon met Paul McCartney at the garden fete (festival) of St Peter's Church, Woolton, Liverpool. Religions are born that way.

7 July 2016, Thursday

Played through all of the 8-string baritone etudes today, which was pleasing, although there are only five of them so far: Inspiration for new etudes has been elusive. Still, I'm not going to force new ones. The five etudes I do have are very good and developed organically, from playing the instrument, listening to what it had to say, and following the Muse. The same is true for the composition and revisions of the *Halloween* pieces. So in lieu of new music, I also practiced some Jaco Pastorius songs as well as a few jazz etudes arranged by Joe Diorio and Bret Willmott, and played a few bluegrass tunes (always good for maintaining and improving speed).

11 July 2016, Monday

Worked on two Zeppelin songs for this Saturday's concert. "Friends" made more sense once I slowed it down and mapped it out. Also, after a bit of counting and cogitating, the intro to "Celebration Day" has become comprehensible with the understanding that it is characteristically Jimmy Page-haphazardness played in an opening tuning. Performance solution: count to four, play what feels good, and explode into the main riff on the downbeat.

14 July 2016, Thursday

Just finished up a tremendously rewarding lesson with a new student who heard that I taught "weird guitar lessons". He recently discovered the 1980s incarnation of King Crimson but couldn't find any lessons or sheet music online. I happily showed him a few of their approaches, the idiosyncratic nature of Robert Fripp's compositions and Adrian Belew's oddball techniques and use of effects. I also gave him some Crimson sheet music I had transcribed and directed him to Belew's *Electronic Guitar* instructional video on YouTube. Additionally, I made sure he was aware of, what is in my opinion, the apex of Crimson's prodigious output, their 1973-74 recordings *Larks Tongue in Aspic*, *Starless And Bible Black* (a life changing record for me), and *Red*. I was thrilled with the look on his face when the reckless precision of "Facture" and "Starless" animated the air around us. And finally I turned him on to some Balinese gamelan music, which inspired the polyrhythmic nature of many '80s Crimson songs. It was an idyllic lesson.

One thing though, this student kept using the term "avant-garde" to describe King Crimson's music as well as my own playing. I had to sportively take umbrage with this phrase: While I can see how the term might apply to a few Crimson songs, I personally don't think I play avant-garde music.

I Don't Play Avant-Garde Music

Although I am often labeled as such, I am not an avant-garde musician. In fact, I don't think there is such thing as avant-garde music any more. Avant-garde, in relation to art, used to mean "cutting edge" and "progressive"; the etymology is French, literally "advance guard" – in a military sense, the first line of troops. Music, in my opinion, hasn't been avant-garde since the 1950s. One can argue that a few 1960s albums such as *Revolver* or *Trout Mask Replica*, or flourishing practices like free improvisation and computer-generated music were avant-garde but you can find all the alleged innovative ideas that are prevalent in those works in recordings from the 1950s, if not earlier.

Sun Ra was experimenting with group (and free) improvisation in the 1950s – hints of his more radical, soon to come, ideas are available on *Super-Sonic Jazz*. (Goodness, if I wanted to stretch it, I could mention Dixieland music laying the foundation for group improvisation in the early 1900s!)

Raymond Scott, whose most famous composition "Powerhouse" found its way into countless Looney Tunes cartoons (and Rush's "La Villa Strangiato"), was also an electronic music pioneer, inventing and recording with ring modulators, envelope filters, and even electronic drum generators in the 1950s.

Even rock and roll was avant-garde in the 1950s. The intentionally distorted guitar amps of Ike Turner and Paul Burlison (guitarist for Johnny Burnette and the Rock and Roll Trio) synthesized a radical sound, one that was, prior to their recordings, to be avoided. A few blues musicians also recorded with distorted tones around the same time as Turner and Burlison, most notably Pat Hare (listen to his stunning playing on James Cotton's "Cotton Crop Blues") and Willie Johnson (with Howlin' Wolf). However it's impossible to know who among them was doing it deliberately, as Turner and Burlison did, and who was a beneficiary/victim of poor equipment.

Two last words on the 1950s and the avant-garde: John Cage.

Today, avant-garde is as generic a term as blues, jazz, or metal. Unfortunately it's a catchall that, to the uninitiated, means anything that isn't commercial – especially if it is weird, dissonant, or cacophonous. Synonymous appellations – experimental, progressive, fringe, forward-thinking, outsider, etc. – do no better at accurately describing the array of styles found under the leaky umbrella of "avant-garde".

The semantics and pigeonholing gets worse: If a musician does label his or her music avant-garde, so that a mainstream audience can understand the music in context, other musicians, who a mainstream audience might also deem avant-garde, will say, "Your music isn't avant-garde! People were doing that 50 years ago!" Damned if you do, and damned if you don't.

70

As an alternative I came up with the term "Modern Primitive Guitar" to describe my guitar playing and composition style [for more see Appendix II]. I have since broadened that moniker to "Modern Primitive Acoustic Scientist Music" so as to include any non-guitar music I compose. These labels are not helpful in any pragmatic sense but they are more playful and emblematic (and less loaded) than avant-garde.

16 July 2016, Saturday

EXERCISE:
ATTEMPT TO DEVELOP QUALITATIVE AESTHETIC CRITERIA FOR ART

"We went out to Utah…a Western house, big rooms, high ceilings…huge windows, that at first you think is bad art and then you see it's great scenery."
- Garrison Keillor*

During debates regarding "good" music versus "bad" music I regularly say – with conviction and a sincere belief – that, "[Insert song title] is not a good song." If this is true then I should be able to provide evidence and, if not facts, standards for my point of view.

Quality As A Hierarchy

Art can be labeled good or bad, but is that a spectrum or a hierarchy? If it exists in a hierarchy, then what follows is a simplified attempt to provide aesthetic criteria for what distinguishes one piece of art as better than another**.

---

* Keillor, Garrison "Blue Plastic", *Local Man Moves To The City*

** This list is additive: Any criteria "Art" possesses will also be inherent in the other three elevated categories; and so forth.

Criteria For Art, Good Art, Great Art, Timeless Art

Art: Anything anyone creates that the creator labels as "art". Food, clothes, drawings, children's art, movies, handsome cabs, sky writing, furniture, car engines, bridges, billboards, toothbrushes, toothbrush packaging, anything.

Good Art: Anything anyone creates that the creator labels as art, that someone else also thinks is art.

Great Art: Art that, more than eliciting a polite "I like it", sincerely moves a person (other than the artist) emotionally; art that, when put into context, has historical value; art that has layers and hidden meanings that can be detected by the observer or sincerely explained by the artist.

Timeless Art: Art that generation after generations keep coming back to; art that doesn't have to be put into historical perspective; art that speaks for itself – in other words, one shouldn't need to read the back-story or artist's statement of intent to find value in it.

Qualities To Be Taken Into Consideration When Evaluating The Aesthetics Of Music

- ❖ Rhythm

- ❖ Melody

- ❖ Harmony (chord progressions and voicings)

- ❖ Lyrical Content

- ❖ Performance

- ❖ Intention

- ❖ Expression

- ❖ Articulation

- ❖ Dynamics

- ❖ Feel

- ❖ Predictability vs. Unpredictability (concerning such matters as lyrics; what beats melody notes and chords fall on; rhythmic performance; etc.)

- ❖ Form and Arrangement

- ❖ Instrumentation

- ❖ Timbre

- ❖ Tone

- ❖ Phrasing

- ❖ Emotional (Intuitive) vs. Intellectual Content

- ❖ Space (or lack thereof)

- ❖ Context (historical and cultural)

Ambiguity And Contradiction

For many years I have maintained that, "Great Art" contains two elements: Ambiguity and Contradiction*.

---

* For example the "primitive" art of trained painters such as Jean Dubuffet, Asger Jorn, and Pablo Picasso; the equivocal ending of Woody Allen's *Manhattan*; and the entire musical output of the KLF.

On the other hand, I'm not fond of art that is either superficial to the point of banality, or so abstract that one has to read about it to understand it – if meaning is so obvious or obscure as to be almost absent, I'm not interested.

I prefer art that, upon first encounter, impels me to think, "I like that. It's intriguing. There is something there; something deeper than the obvious." Then, when/if I do research the work and encounter it a second, third, or hundredth time, and think, "Wow, I didn't see that before. It's different this time, yet still effective. I like it." That is great art.

17 July 2016, Sunday

Last night, I, along with a first rate band, performed all of *Led Zeppelin III* at a benefit concert. The performances were commendable. I was quite pleased with my solo on "Since I've Been Loving You", which was dynamic and tasteful, if flashier that I usually play (if you're going to imitate Jimmy Page you better be flamboyant), and aided by my secret weapon, panning delay.

18 July 2016, Monday

An excellent R.O.E.* rehearsal last night. One curious aspect: If you had asked me what tribute bands I would have agreed to play in, I would have listed a thousand others before I ever considered Jackson Browne. I liked his hits, "Somebody's Baby", "Doctor My Eyes", and Nico's version of "These Days", but I was unfamiliar with his other songs. In fact, I had never heard 8 of the 17 songs in our set until last December (when this band was organized).

---

* In addition to Jackson Browne, this group also plays material from the catalogue of the "Laurel Canyon sound" – the music of the Eagles, Bonnie Raitt, Linda Ronstadt, and my personal favorite, Warren Zevon.

20 July 2016, Wednesday

FAST FOOD MUSIC

I have no problem with fast food. Not as a concept, not as means of sustenance, not as commercial enterprise. I don't frequent fast food restaurants, though I do sporadically take my kids to one of them because they enjoy playing in the indoor playground, getting a toy with their meals, and – least important – eating the food.

I also know that fast food is not fine dining; most of the food is arguably only half-good and half-healthy. People shouldn't eat it everyday. I know this. You know this. And, I hope, even fast food owners and employees know this. This is why I have no problem with fast food.

Top 40, sugar-sweet pop songs are the fast food of music.

Correlation: I have no problem with Top 40, sugar-sweet pop songs. However, if you offer me a pop song with trite songwriting and formulaic production, then scheme to dress it up as art – of which the most frequent commercial manifestations are to play it on acoustic guitar, inveigle the lyrics with a patina of solemnity, and clothe the performer in the uniform of the steadfast, noble everyman (threadbare, faded t-shirt; torn and dirty blue jeans; tattered but rakish fedora, Breton, or cowboy hat) –, and promote it in a somber, grainy, sepia tone video; well now, now I'm angry.

All of the above is analogous to me going into a fine restaurant – with expensive and discriminating décor, well-dressed and well-mannered employees – and ordering the special, only to be brought a McDonald's happy meal on a china plate with sterling silverware. Do not try to deceive me! I will eat fast food off a paper wrapper, in a plastic booth, with a sticky floor; but don't contrive to serve it to me as credible nourishment in a five star bistro.

Sigh. Today one of my favorite students asked to learn a "new" song by a popular female folk-rock entertainer. Within six seconds of listening – no exaggeration, SIX SECONDS! – I heard a song I've encountered a thousand times before, including a wholesale rip-off of the opening figure of "Blackbird" by The Beatles. The song is fine. It has a verse and a chorus, a chord progression and a melody, and lyrics…ugh…those Disney-esque lyrics, contrived to create the illusion of sincere sadness, untimely loss, or undying love. The song is a jingle pretending to be art.

Please stop. Please, please stop. At least own up to what you are, a sheep in sheep's clothing.

But these musical fast food phonies will never stop trying to trick us, there's too much to gain. So what to do about it?

76

As a private music teacher I've always thought it was my job to provide students with not only what I think is best but also, and more importantly, with what they want. The lessons are not about me, they are about the student. If students want to learn pitiable songs, if that will bring them joy, then I can do that. But perhaps for every pathetically unoriginal song, I need to insist – gently but emphatically – that students also learn of the pioneers and precedents they set. Who knows, maybe the professional musicians I've alluded to aren't phonies; conceivably they're ignorantly derivative because no one stepped in and said, "The emperor wears no clothes!"

21 July 2016, Thursday

I had an excruciating, sadness inducing headache from the time I woke up until the late afternoon. I have suffered from terrible headaches since I was a teenager. So has my father, who had a massive, debilitating stroke at age 55.

If I ever needed a sign that I shouldn't do a job I don't enjoy, then my father's stroke was that sign (Not that I needed one. And I would give almost anything for my father to not have had that stroke.). It makes me sad to write about it. My father retired from a mid-level job with the U.S. Government in his early 50s, did some part-time consulting, bought his dream car – a Corvette, a car he'd longed for since before he could drive –, and had a stroke four months later. He never drove that car again.

23 July 2016, Saturday

Performing this "safe" music – played by the '80s cover band and the Jackson Browne tribute band – leaves me slightly wanting, even though the audiences for these groups has been considerably larger than for any of my personal musical projects (Boud Deun, Prester John, or my solo work).

Jackson Browne, the Eagles, Madonna, they all write and record solid songs. But they're a bit too polished for my taste. I need contrast. I don't want to listen exclusively to safe music all night. Every song is similar, smooth, nothing jarring, nothing radical, just good. I don't want just good. I want the unexpected! It's one of the many things I loved about playing with David Miller in Prester John: We habitually juxtaposed pop and weird music, performing a catchy, three-chord, storytelling song immediately following or proceeding a complex, semi-abstract, atonal instrumental. No wonder we were so popular.

Halloween follows a comparable modus operandi – more or less alternating weird pieces with almost-normal ones. These descriptions are relative of course. I find very little of *Halloween* to be weird, excepting "Seven, The Magic Number (Plus Or Minus Two)" – of which a friend of mine, after hearing a MIDI demo, said, "It sounds like Captain Beefheart went to finishing school." That made me happy. Nevertheless, I know my perspective is skewed; *Halloween* is at least fifty percent weird, whether I believe so or not.

Acknowledging my perspective – or lack thereof – reminds me of something Mat Eiland (Boud Deun bassist) once said when we were in the studio listening to a playback of his song "Waterford".

"This part is so groovy," he whooped with delight, "you can really dance to it."

I responded more realistically, "Mat, you couldn't dance to this song unless you had three legs and one of them was longer than the others!"

Mat kept dancing.

Twenty-First Century Folk Music

I had an interesting experience with a student this morning. We were recording two songs he had written, both with strong melodic movement and imaginative, storytelling lyrics. After we recorded the basic guitar tracks, I had him perform several vocal takes, working on delivery and tonal consistency. We also edited his lyrics, getting rid of superfluous words and syllables, such as "but", "and", the "be" in "because", and consonants at the end of words – such as the "d" in "said" and the "g" in "running".

When we were finished I felt we had something very good, not mind-blowingly original, and not something that was likely to get played on the radio today, but admirable. It later occurred to me that what we had recorded was folk music. Now it didn't sound like the "folk music" idiom, in fact the songs were more akin to Joe Jackson circa 1979, but it was definitely *genuine* folk music: Music for the people and by the people.

I kept thinking, if this was 100 years ago he would have sung this song to his family and friends, maybe even his co-workers. His friends and acquaintances would play instruments or sing along because more people used to sing, play instruments, and understand the basics mechanics of music (if we can believe this popular legend about the "olden days"). Music was more of an equalizer 100 years ago, not the imbalanced performer/audience dichotomy we have today. Recording this song would not have been an option 100 years ago. It would have existed as a one-time live event (multiple live events if those around him wanted to hear it again). And his vocal ability wouldn't have been judged in the same way that we evaluate singing today.

Songs by an amateur writer don't have to be momentous or incomparable. In this case, "good" is good enough. This student contributed to my life today with his song. It moved me. He was creating something unique unto himself; though I also felt he was expressing something, something outside of himself, which needed to be expressed. It was positive and constructive. But I think if he put that song up for sale online I wouldn't enjoy it as much. It was good because he did it for himself. Then he shared it with me. It wasn't for money or fame. It was an example of pure creation. I am grateful to have been part of this experience.

27 July 2016, Wednesday

THE HARMING POWER OF MUSIC?

I've encountered many authors who talk tirelessly about the healing power of music but no one, as far as I've found, ever talks about how music can harm. I don't mean the way certain types of music can stir up aggression; what I'm talking about is music that incites frustration, queasiness, chagrin, and, at its most benign, disappointment. What is happening in the brain and body when those feelings arise from listening to particular songs? Did Oliver Sacks do experiments of this type? Has anyone? As it turns out: Yes...kind of.

Today I had a thought-provoking phone conversation with neuroscientist Dr. Robert Zatorre, researcher at Montreal Neurological Institute and a professor at McGill University, who has conducted (and written about) many experiments on how human brains react to music (genuine neurological reactions) regarding emotional ranges such as:

❖ Pleased – Displeased

❖ Irritated – Untroubled

❖ Angry – Calm

❖ Bored – Interested

❖ Tense – Relaxed

All of which can be measured empirically. Unfortunately, "why" the brain reacts as such cannot be explained precisely because there are a myriad of wide-ranging factors to be considered, from emotional to social, memory based to reward based, biological to specific sonic stimuli – and those are just the basics. As I suspected, the interview produced more questions than answers.

Nonetheless, Dr. Zatorre did describe some studies that shed scientific light on reasons why some people, like myself, enjoy unusual, unpredictable, and highly dissonant music. Two specific reasons are musical training (seems obvious enough, though not all musically trained individuals enjoy unusual, unpredictable, and highly dissonant music) and a personality trait* that neuroscientists label "openness to experience". Someone who scores high on openness to experience would, tend to welcome "less conventional styles of music" [Dr. Zatorre's words]. As opposed to most mainstream, commercial music that would be considered "conventional", and preferred by people who score low on "openness to experience"**.

Final conclusion regarding my interview with Dr. Zatorre: There are many things we don't know about the feelings that we attach to music, but we can know *why* we don't know, and that is a step towards understanding.

---

* Wikipedia contributors. "Trait theory." Wikipedia, The Free Encyclopedia, July 27, 2016: "In psychology, trait theory (also called dispositional theory) is an approach to the study of human personality. Trait theorists are primarily interested in the measurement of *traits*, which can be defined as habitual patterns of behavior, thought, and emotion. According to this perspective, traits are relatively stable over time, differ across individuals (e.g. some people are outgoing whereas others are shy), and influence behavior. Traits are in contrast to states, which are more transitory dispositions.

In some theories and systems, traits are something a person either has or does not have, but in many others traits are dimensions such as extraversion vs. introversion, with each person rating somewhere along this spectrum."

** Regarding the range of "openness to experience" scores, this should not be misconstrued as a positive or negative personality characteristic, but more akin to safe vs. adventurous or spontaneous vs. deliberate.

EXERCISE: CREATE A MUSICAL SPECTRUM

My discussion with Dr. Zatorre got me thinking about my 16 July 2016 exercise, "Attempt To Develop Qualitative Aesthetic Criteria for Art". In that exercise I endeavored to look at the various qualities of art as a hierarchy. But what if I look at these qualities as a spectrum of taste instead, as trait theory suggests that for many traits – such as openness to experience – most people will rate somewhere along a spectrum and not fall into an all-or-nothing category.

Create a musical spectrum from 1, "safe", to 100, "adventurous". This is not a spectrum of bad to good but of personal taste. My spectrum would look like this:

❖ At 1 I would place children's music, "Twinkle, Twinkle Little Star", "Frere Jacques", etc. Simple songs that serve a valuable purpose but most adults probably are not eager to listen to for pleasure.

❖ At 100 I would place the composed, highly complex, academic, un-catchy, and, arguably, unlistenable music of the 20th Century, such as the academic concert music of twelve-tone row serialism. This is experimental music but, in my personal opinion, experiments that fail. Again, most adults probably aren't eager to listen to this for fun.

❖ At 25 would be most contemporary country music.

❖ Right in the middle, at 50, I would place the Eagles, Kenny Rodgers, Carly Simon.

❖ 49 Bonnie Raitt, 51 Bon Jovi, 52 Tom Petty, 53 Bob Marley, 57 The Beach Boys, 80 *The Symphonic Dances of West Side Story* and *The Firebird Suite*, etc.

❖ Once the spectrum is established, circle your preferences. What type of music do you like? Is it safe, middle-of-the-road, or adventurous?

Was this useful? Maybe not. There's nothing objective about making your own spectrum. But does anyone think the Eagles are adventurous? Maybe. I suppose people will have to share and compare their lists with others. If my two exercises regarding taste have proven anything, it is that attempting to establish an aesthetic criterion for art is probably impossible but the endeavor is useful for personal perspective.

28 July 2016, Thursday

The curse of having listened to a lot of music, across genres, is that you've "heard it all before." I'll value music that sounds similar to something I've heard previously if kids in a basement or garage play it. But when people spend lots of money on production and packaging, and then market this kids' basement music – as played by adults – as innovative, something is wrong.

So, can I point this critical finger at myself? How does *Halloween* measure up? Rather than claiming that *Halloween* is anything new (though I do believe it is unique), I'll gladly acknowledge my influences. Or rather, since the inspirations are countless, I'll point out the most pervasive ones:

❖ The Kronos Quartet – in the mid-1990s I was obsessed with their 1986 self-titled recording featuring pieces by Peter Sculthorpe, Conlon Nancarrow, and Philip Glass, which, ipso facto, are also *Halloween* influences

❖ Thelonious Monk – I'm constantly revisiting his mischievous melodies, syncopated rhythms, and oddball yet delectable harmonies

❖ George Martin's string arrangements for The Beatles ("Eleanor Rigby" is hiding in almost every piece in *Halloween*)

❖ Béla Bartók's string quartets

❖ Tchaikovsky's long-form, playful, dance melodies

❖ Patsy Cline – though her influence might not be apparent in playing, I endeavored to put Patsy's perspicacious, yet searching, phrasing into my performance of the *Halloween* melodies

30 July 2016, Saturday

Am I procrastinating or waiting for the perfect time (October) to record *Halloween*? October is not only symbolic but I have also found that my acoustic guitars sound their best in October and November. I've concluded this is because here in Connecticut both the barometric pressure and humidity are at the perfect level in autumn. The summer is too humid, winter is too dry, spring is too capricious, autumn is just right. So I'm pretending that that is why I haven't recorded anything yet. We'll see what October brings.

31 July 2016, Sunday

"Etude No. 6" coalesced today, with the simplest of stratagem: I followed the first seven measures' descending, though displaced, chromatic scale (an idea that has been lingering in my compositional purgatory for a year) with a variation in which I play each note twice, in different registers, instead of once. This outrageously straightforward amendment was so effective that with the addition of just seven measures and 26 notes, the etude was completed.

Although this etude doesn't coincide specifically with Pauline Oliveros' "Deep Listening"* concepts, "Deep Listening" did influence this piece, as well as etudes No. 1 and 2. For instance, because the "8" has such a long decay time and the overtones ring to high heaven, there is this constant fluctuation of dissonance and consonance as the fundamental and overtones of each note sustain and overlap. To hear the full effect of these harmonies, the etude needs to be performed at a snail's pace. Even once I stop playing, the "8" continues, as the last five notes ring out in a glorious cluster of sonic uncertainty.

---

* For more on Pauline Oliveros and Deep Listening visit www.paulineoliveros.us and www.deeplistening.org/site/

AUGUST

2 August 2016, Tuesday

I LIKE SHORT SONGS

I've begun the process of rereading all the passages I've underlined in books I've previously read. Today's noteworthy passage is from Ben Shahn's *The Shape of Content*:

> A small sketch of Picasso's, a drawing of Rouault, or Manet or Modigliani is not to be dismissed as negligible, for any such piece contains inevitably the long evolutionary process of taste, deftness, and personal view. It is, in brief, still dictated by the same broad experience and personal understanding which mold the larger work. [p. 40]

I rarely feel a need for external validation (I am brimming with self-confidence endowed by my loving parents) but I do value thoughtful like-mindedness, especially when it concerns an uncommon perspective. Shahn's words are corroborating evidence of my belief in the importance of composing very short pieces of music.

I have composed, recorded, and released at least a dozen pieces that clock in at less than one minute. *Halloween* is now proving to serve as an archetype for this style of composing, as it is made up of 13 different pieces, but the total length will probably be under 24 minutes! Three pieces in *Halloween* are less than a minute in length, and six more are less than two minutes. Still, these pieces say all they have to say – and they say quite a bit.

For many years I have maintained that longer works aren't better, they're just longer. Many a 20-40-minute classical symphony is composed of obligatory filler. As Igor Stravinsky is reputed to have said, "Too many pieces of music finish too long after the end." This is not to say that there aren't long works in which each note serves a purpose, only that one shouldn't judge the value of a piece of music by how many notes it has or how long it is…

I was going to write, "how long it takes to listen to it" but in fact that might be a more accurate measure of its worth. An intriguing 32-second piece of music might excite a listener to play it over and over and over again, turning those 32 seconds into an hour or more. Conversely, many a listener would be hard-pressed to listen to a pretty-good 90-minute symphony more than once in one sitting.

3 August 2016, Wednesday

Spent most of the day on a train to Virginia transcribing an interview I recently conducted with Dream Theater guitarist John Petrucci for *Wood&Steel*. Petrucci was a polished interviewee, candid and appropriately loquacious. This will be my first published interview. Though I did interview bluegrass/newgrass guitarist Larry Keel 10 years ago for *Guitar Player*, but that ended up as a profile, not as a verbatim interview. (Side note: Keel and I attended the same high school, at the same time, but never met! For a small town in rural Virginia, our school was outrageously overcrowded.)

5 August 2016, Saturday

MUSIC VS. SPECTACLE

Last night my kids and I went to an outdoor concert on the Hamden Green to see/hear a Bruce Springsteen tribute band. The lead singer sounded exactly like Bruce Springsteen and the band was tight, but the whole situation seemed peculiar, empty, and decidedly "uncool". The audience was a disappointment as well: indifferent couples and overstressed parents, determined to enjoy a low-cost night out, sitting in lawns chairs, swatting flies, half-listening. It made me feel a little uncomfortable considering my role in the '80s cover band (nothing new there) and R.O.E. At least none of the singers in R.O.E. are trying to sound like Jackson Browne. (I'm not trying to justify what that band does, merely explaining that R.O.E. is a celebration of the music, not an attempt to recreate the vocal performances note-for-note.)

Being in this sprawling outdoor setting also made me realize that I have been to very few concerts such as this one. These shows are not necessarily about music; they are "events", possibly even spectacles, in which music plays only a small part. Since such a happening doesn't concisely define itself (is it an event, spectacle, or music performance?), never fulfilling any one goal, I find them, ironically, one-dimensional.

Perhaps I've been to the wrong (or not enough) concerts so my perspective is limited: What "big" concerts have I been to? Sammy Hagar and Krokus; The Firm; Power Station; Sting; A Gathering of the Tribes featuring X, Fishbone, Primus, Steve Earle, EPMD, King's X, Salt-N-Pepa, and John Wesley Harding; Steely Dan; and The Police.

Not many. And all of the above, excepting the first two, are rather unmemorable in any moving or life-affirming sense: I have more criticisms than endorsements for such events.

Most of the concerts I have attended (and my favorites) have been in smaller venues – ranging from freezing cold inner city parking garages to cozy house concerts in the suburbs, sweaty punk basements to plush performing arts venues. And many of these shows had ridiculously meager audience attendance.

I wonder how many concerts have I attended? I'd say about 120. I'm no doubt forgetting a few, but let's say that's four shows a year since I was 15. That doesn't sound like many; I have friends who attend a show a week.

What does this tell me?

Though the numbers aren't staggering, I have attended plenty of shows, in just about every genre, so it's not a lack of broad-ranging experiences that's informing my opinions of the live concert experience.

I can see that I've missed a few of the "classic live bands", such as U2, KISS, Led Zeppelin (before my time), The Rolling Stones, Paul McCartney, The Grateful Dead, Van Halen, and Metallica. However, I feel I can safely say that those types of arena concerts are events and spectacles, not necessarily purely musical experiences. Which is fine, but not what I'm interested in. So...

What do I want from live music?

Energy: But not energy that has been dissipated from having traveled through large crowds. Arguably a good, large crowd can generate even more energy, but, in my experience, this doesn't usually happen; and if it does, this energy is not necessarily musical, it is the energy of crowds: If I was to be overly cynical I would suggest the energy of "mobs".

I want to feel the energy from the vibrations of the notes (and I don't mean decibel volume); the energy of the performer(s); and the energy of an audience with mutual objectives, which are to listen to the music, enjoy it, absorb it, appreciate it, make contact with it, but not to willfully interfere with it (on this last point I'm thinking of the uncalled for "Freebird" request or insincere "Woo!" echoing from the back of the room after every song).

Clarity and Symbiosis: I am aware of the contradiction here: "clarity" implies I want to discern every note, which I do, but "symbiosis" implies I want to hear all the notes working together as one. This is one of the ultimate powers and paradoxes of exceptional music. Whether it is Leo Kottke playing solo, Shoutbus playing as a trio, or 80 musicians playing as an orchestra, the best performances allow me to focus on both the forest and the trees at the same time.

Authenticity: This could be the raw, visceral authenticity of teenagers playing in a basement or the cultivated authenticity of Leo Kottke or Larry Coryell. It is not the insincere authenticity of a stadium band pulling an audience member up on stage because they know it will elicit a reaction from the crowd. That is pandering and the last thing I want from a live music experience.

Talent/Skill/Ability/Craft: These are all slightly different but for now I'll say, I need performers to provide me with something I can admire and be motivated by. This can be the technical skill of an instrumentalist – Billy Cobham or Mike Keneally; the songwriting craft of an average player – Johnny Cash or Pete Townshend; a natural singing ability enhanced by years of onstage performance – Paul McCartney, Bon Scott, or Patsy Cline; or the indefinable X factor that infuses the delivery of a line or even a physical gesture with mysterious poignancy, here I'm thinking more about comedians and actors than musicians – Woody Allen or Steve Martin – but I've seen Ray Davies, Junior Brown, Jeff Beck, The Smothers Brothers, and Victor Borge do this too (obviously Borge and The Smothers Brothers straddle the music/comedy border).

I had a teacher at Musicians Institute who was the quintessential curmudgeon, but every now and then he would say something profound. A student once asked his opinion regarding the music of one of his more famous contemporaries. Without missing a beat the curmudgeon-turned-sage said, "He's in show business. I'm in the music business." That about sums it up.

93

8 August 2016, Monday

Today I spent hours (seriously hours!) practicing the slide articulations I have to perform on the nylon during in the **C** section of *Halloween* "Two…"

These slides are outrageously tricky to actualize but they're fundamental to the part…even if they did appear by accident. You see, when I originally made MIDI files of these parts, I assigned a "classical guitar" sound to this track. Unbeknownst to me the MIDI sound played everything with slides! This produced a wonderful effect, however I found it impossible to replicate it in the **A** and **B** sections – they are too fast and technically demanding – but for the **C** section the melody is just sparse enough to allow me to reproduce the technique, or strive to anyway. That's what I spent hours on today!

9 August 2016, Tuesday

Another valuable quote from Ben Shahn's *The Shape of Content*:

> The artist occupies a unique position vis-à-vis the society in which he lives. However dependent upon it he may be for his livelihood, he is still somewhat removed from its immediate struggles for social status or for economic supremacy. He has no really vested interest in the status quo. [p. 79]

In many ways I consider this characterization to be one of the main ingredients of a true artist, as compared to a performer or a craftsman: All three vocations are essential to culture, civilization, and an expansion of consciousness, but each possesses different abilities and, most particularly, aims.

Faith In The Future Of Music

I like to believe that a new "popular" music will arise in just a few more years. By then, perchance 2020-2030 (changes in musical trends usually suffer a latent period only quantifiable in hindsight, so my time frame is merely a guess), musicians and audiences will have had time to reevaluate music's role in contemporary culture. By then music may find a new and rewarding place in a world dominated by computer technology that encourages musical creativity and innovation as well as a symbiotic relationship between all genres and technologies. And I don't mean the predictable combination of music and images – soundtracks, background music, or videos – or computer programs that allow people to "compose" in a cut-and-paste or paint-by-numbers form. I'm suggesting pioneering ideas and applications – something unknown and unforeseen right now. I find this prospect exciting.

My hope for something new means musicians are obliged to study and learn from the old masters, whether that be The Beatles, Jimi Hendrix, Janis Joplin; Bach, Mozart, Beethoven; Louis Armstrong, Miles Davis, Henry Threadgill; Woody Guthrie, Nina Simone, Paul Simon; John Cage, Pauline Oliveros, Laurie Anderson; Ravi Shankar, Nusrat Ali Khan, Habib Koité; or, best and perhaps most vital, all of the above*. Because, although innovation can be born of ignorance – there are historical accounts of amateurs and outsiders providing naïve but effective solutions to complex problems – these are exceptions. More often innovation stems from knowledge of what has come before and educated risks.

13 August 2016, Saturday

Played a dance last night with The Luck Pushers in a stiflingly hot church (90 degrees at 9pm) converted into a community center – with all of nine people in attendance. It was fantastic! Everyone had a ball. And though we cut the evening short, it was a night of excellent music and (if I do say so myself) inspired guitar solos – I felt incorporeal, listening to the music instead of playing it.

---

* My ideal music for the 21st century: A band that combines the excitement, energy, and entertainment value of KISS, The Sex Pistols, Madonna; the technical skill of Glenn Gould, Charlie Parker, Leo Kottke; the artistic integrity of Thelonious Monk, John Fahey, Robert Fripp; the incorporation of World music in a way that isn't pastiche or overtly derivative; and most important of all, the songwriting ability of The Beatles, Paul Simon, and Carol King – without a solid foundation and understanding of songwriting I think much of the rest will be useless.

15 August 2016, Monday

I finally figured out what to do with the groove in *Halloween* "Ten..." Up to this point the entire piece has been alternating measures of 3/4 and 4/4. When the MIDI plays it back it works, but when I've demoed the parts live there is absolutely no groove. It's super stiff. So today I modified the baritone guitar riff so that the intro still alternates 3/4 - 4/4 but when the melody comes in the riff switches to a straight 4/4 feel (all I had to do was add one more note); this made the piece much groovier. I hear the drums from James Brown's "Cold Sweat" all over this (that dynamite syncopation when Clyde Stubblefield skips the downbeat and pops the snare on the "and" of four instead). After recording a few passes of the melody over this new feel, the steel-string has started beseeching me to give it a more rhythmically diverse counter-melody (currently it plays a meager variation of the nylon's melody): I can feel the need for this but I don't hear it. Tomorrow I hope to get more comfortable with this new feel and try some fresh melodic ideas on the steel-string.

17 August 2016, Wednesday

Top secret: Yesterday I was told that Taylor Guitars is going to start making a GS Mini bass (the GS Mini model is a popular, small-bodied acoustic guitar made by Taylor). Taylor hasn't made *any* kind of bass guitar for several years and used ones are expensive ($3,000 and up), so this news excites me greatly. Having an acoustic bass would open up new possibilities for *Halloween*. And even though I probably won't be able to get my hands on one until January of next year, I'm already devising a new arrangement of *Halloween*.

Using a bass to play the lowest parts of *Halloween*, instead of the 8-string baritone, will allow me to avoid key transposition for the baritone (the baritone is tuned a fourth lower than a guitar – or a fifth higher than a bass, depending on your perspective), which will make scoring much easier. This bass alternative will also give more people access to the low parts of *Halloween*…Hmmm…this is not something I've written about, the fact that I want *Halloween* to become standard repertoire for guitar ensembles. No time like the present…

There are a multitude of logistical issues surrounding the recording of *Halloween* (not to mention the composing) that require that I play all four guitar parts myself. And while I will admit that this is in part an artistic compulsion, ultimately it is a pragmatic consideration. However, I do consider *Halloween* an ensemble work and I have faith that it will some day be performed live, with four different guitarists.

It is also my hope that *Halloween* will encourage guitarists to play together in a new way. I know from experience that there is an abundance of guitarists throughout the world. Most of these guitarists, when they play together (if they do play together), tend to stick to the traditional roles of accompanist or soloist. I am all for this! I support and encourage it. Still, I'm optimistic that *Halloween* will point guitarists into further directions, directions that foster group-interaction; active-listening; extreme attention to detail, nuance, dynamics, articulation, timbre, etc.; and camaraderie.

24 August 2016, Wednesday

Tonight I played my final show with the '80s cover band. It was fine; comparable to all the other shows this band has played. As a finale it was appropriately anti-climatic.

Before the show, the soundman was playing formulaic, contemporary country music over the P.A. – before the "80's show". I felt like saying, "Would you mind playing something less polarizing?" But if there is one thing I have learned playing live music it is this: Always be nice to the soundman.

One thing I will miss about this band is the opportunity to play songs by one-hit-wonders. I love such songs as "867-5309" by Tommy Tutone, "Take on Me" by A-ha, and "Video Killed the Radio Star" by The Buggles, because these one-hit wonders often wear the façade of formulaic songwriting but upon further investigation one finds uniqueness and care in the productions: Akin to the work of a lapidary – enough shaping and polish without diminishing the equivocal essence of inspiration. Perhaps that's why originators of one-hit wonders find follow-up success nearly impossible. The first song is original but most subsequent recordings are pale imitations.

25 August 2016, Thursday

It's dawning on me that recording *Halloween* is going to be a massive – and slightly daunting – undertaking. There are only 13 *Halloween* pieces, but each piece has four parts, consequently there are 52 parts to learn! Feasibly, that is hours of music to perform and record.

28 August 2016, Sunday

DOO WOP NIGHT

Last night The Luck Pushers played a country club gig that was uneven and frustrating for several reasons.

We had been hired to play "Doo Wop Night" and I had told the entertainment director that we did in fact have the repertoire for such a gig; or rather I said that we would be playing a touch of doo wop but primarily the music would be 1950s rock and roll, with some Beatles' songs thrown in to broaden the scope. I even sent a copy of the set list to the entertainment board for approval.

Unfortunately, during the performance one club member kept nitpicking our song selection: "Play more doo wop; this is Beatles." So we sang Dion's "Runaround Sue", in three-part harmony, followed by Elvis, Carl Perkins, and Chuck Berry.

Later, as we performed a Latin twist version of "Besame Mucho", the same club member loudly complained, "What song are they playing? We can't dance to this." So after "Besame…" we switched back to some swing-based 1950s rock and roll.

One final time the same grump asked for "Something slow, so the older people can dance." So we played "Fly Me To The Moon", which is not rock and roll or doo wop, but it was originally recorded in 1954 (by Kaye Ballard) and it is slow.

I should point out that this one member was the only person complaining (a fledging Judge Smails); many others were dancing and having a grand time. But here is a problem I have: When I'm hired to provide specific music, I aim to please *everyone*. And regrettably I let this one malcontent distract me from all the other pleased and happy people. It spoiled the gig for me. I take full responsibility for this; there is no one to blame but myself. And, annoyingly, it is also possible this complainer's criticism was valid.

This morning I searched online for "best doo wop" songs and received a lesson in both musical semantics and music history that I should have learned a long time ago:

I always considered doo wop to be vocal-harmony based, multi-voiced, street-corner music sung by black musicians, that found its way into recording studios about a year before rock and roll clicked – that is to say, before Chuck Berry recorded "Maybellene" in 1955. Songs such as "Sh-Boom" by

The Chords (1954) and "Earth Angel" by The Penguins (1954) are, in my opinion, the quintessential doo wop songs. By 1955-56, after "rock and roll" became an accepted label for the music of Chuck Berry, Little Richard, Jerry Lee Lewis, et al., doo wop was absorbed as a subgenre of rock and roll. Doo wop based rock and roll was smoother, with an emphasis on the vocal harmonies: Prime examples of post-1955 doo wop songs are "Why Do Fools Fall In Love" by Frankie Lymon and The Teenagers, "Searchin'" by The Coasters, and "Come and Go With Me" by The Del-Vikings.

But after my research this morning, I had to broaden my definition of doo wop. Doo wop, in popular culture, appears to be any "light", multi-voiced, vocal-harmony based music sung by black *and* white musicians, and it need not be connected directly to rock and roll. Many of the biggest doo wop hits are slow, romantic, even jazzy, ballads – "Smoke Gets In Your Eyes" by The Platters, "I Only Have Eyes for You" by The Flamingos, and "16 Candles" by The Crests. It appears that doo wop is in fact a genre separate from rock and roll, with its own subgenres – rock-and-roll-doo-wop and pop-doo-wop – not the other way around.

I feel like a fool for not having considered the broad scope of doo wop. I wish I had done a little more research and added a few more songs to The Luck Pushers' repertoire before last night's gig. What it comes down to is that I was under-prepared and that embarrassed me. That one country club member had a legitimate complaint (even if the person was ill-tempered when expressing it); we should have performed a couple of the quintessential doo wop ballads and a few more up-tempo vocal-harmony songs. Even more frustrating is the fact that we could have easily learned these songs with just a bit more rehearsal. In the future, I will do my best to not take for granted such a specific, stylistic, performance opportunity.

SEPTEMBER

PROCRASTINATION VS. COGITATION

I'm preparing to compose and record a new piece of music for a curious compilation CD entitled *Frets of Yore*. The originator/curator of this project is Gonzalo Fuentes, a Chilean artist, musician, and DJ that I connected with about 15 years ago when he started playing my music on his radio show. Here are the original notes and guidelines that Fuentes sent to all the CD contributors:

Frets of Yore: A graphic/music project by Guerrilla Graphics in the form of an international guitar sampler CD.

I will create a folder of 20 Guerrilla Graphics artworks and ask players to contribute a short guitar piece based on one of those 20 artworks. [Note: Fuentes invited other artists to contribute visual works, hence, this project has gone far beyond 20 pieces.]

Each guitar piece should be one to two minutes long, composed or improvised or both. Collage or sound montages are also welcome.

I was immediately drawn to this project, as the visual arts have always been an inspiration for my music [see Appendix II: A Modern Primitive Guitar Primer]. Once I picked the painting I would work from – a semi-abstract, bird's-eye view of a city park, entitled "Mon Parc" by Frederi Lipczyński – I knew instantly what I would compose.

My plan: 1) record random environmental audio in a park, 2) edit that audio and create a soundscape collage that could hold a listener's interest for 30 seconds, 3) compose music that matches the predominant and most intriguing sounds of the soundscape, and 4) mix and arrange the track so listeners will hear the composed music isolated, the soundscape isolated, and then both simultaneously.

Two weeks ago, I took my kids to Dinosaur State Park in Rocky Hill, CT, where I recorded random snippets of audio as we walked around. The park was having a special free event so there were hundreds of people, mostly parents with their kids. Needless to say, it was noisy. These are the environmental recordings* I'm working with and my piece is now titled "Mon (Dinosaur) Parc".

I have probably done 90 minutes of actual hands-on work for this piece; but half of that, the environmental recording, was done more than a month after I formulated my original idea. I then waited another two weeks to edit and assemble the soundscape. And now I'm writing this text before I finally

---

* While writing this entry I searched online for "environmental recordings" as I thought there might be a better term than that or "soundscape" or "musique concrète" for what I'm doing. Alas, I couldn't find one. Though I did learn that composer R. Murray Schafer is credited with coining the term "soundscape".

begin recording the music. Is this procrastination or cogitation?

It's 11:30am: I'm going to start working on the music now.

1:15pm: I've finished the first draft. Not bad, almost two hours of work to compose and arrange 25 seconds of music.

3 September 2016, Saturday

Frank Zappa And Quality vs. Quantity: How Much Art Does An Artist Need To Create?

The past two days were the first in a long time in which I have enjoyed more than three continuous hours of "free time" to work on such a project as yesterday's *Frets of Yore* recording. I don't need to be inspired to do such work, but I do need blocks of time. I'm not bemoaning this lack of time, as I don't feel the need to continuously create – I'm not driven in that way. I'm content with possessing a relatively small but high-quality (in my humble opinion) body of work. This gets me thinking about Frank Zappa.

Frank Zappa was the archetype of an artistic workaholic. Between 1966 and 1993 he released 62 albums: More than two albums a year for 27 years! (Plus, there are 46 posthumous releases.) I unequivocally love and hold in the highest esteem a small amount of Zappa's output. In particular his music from 1972-74 – *Over-Nite Sensation, Apostrophe ('), Roxy & Elsewhere, One Size Fits All, You Can't Do That on Stage Anymore Vol. 2* (released in 1988 but recorded live in 1974), and *The Best Band You Never Heard in Your Life* (disc 1, which features live recordings from 1988 but is primarily material that he composed in the 1970s, essentially a "greatest hits live") – as well as his second album, and masterpiece, *Absolutely Free*. But I find the other 96 percent of Zappa's music to be practically unlistenable! I've done the math here, 7 out of 62 is 4.34 percent (I've not included the posthumous releases in my equation). That little fact (a fact regarding my opinion, but that counts too) prompts a couple of questions:

How does one evaluate an artist's worth if one venerates 5 percent yet finds 95 percent disappointing? I find this easy to answer. The artist is brilliant! I can ignore the bad. We're not talking moral conduct here...are we? No, we are not! Well, well, well...that's a HUGE epiphany! I think I have fallaciously believed that artistic work must have some sort of personal *and* moral significance, but this clearly isn't true. You can be a disagreeable person and still create beautiful art. Or you can be the friendliest person and create dreadful art. You can also be a "normal" person – both disagreeable and kind in any given situation – and create both beautiful and dreadful art. Consistency is almost impossible – otherwise you're a craftsman, not an artist.

Second question: Must an artist produce a surfeit of art in order to create a small amount that is exceptional? I suppose it depends on the artist and the art form. The Beatles are an intriguing, dichotomous point of reference. All 12 official Beatles albums are brilliant; but the individual members, post-Beatles, solo work doesn't come close to measuring up. The Police fit that mold too: Five fantastic albums, then they break up: Excepting Sting's *Dream of the Blue Turtles*, none of their solo albums are comparable in quality to the music of the trio. But that doesn't answer my question.

So how much art does an artist need to create? They *need* to create as much as *needs* to be created. But like all the questions I have recently asked myself regarding art, creativity, and taste, there are no absolutes. Art, taste, quality, even quantity are all subjective and relative. Nevertheless, I do believe that the aesthetic investigations I've gone though to obtain this oversimplified yet ubiquitous answer have demonstrated value beyond the ambivalence of their solutions.

• • •

By the way, today I made my kids a Frank Zappa mix CD. They love "Cheepnis", "Evelyn, a Modified Dog", and "Son of Suzy Creamcheese" – all songs they sing along with in the car – so I think they'll also enjoy, "Call Any Vegetable", "San Ber'dino", and, although arguably inappropriate for their ages (5 and 7), "Don't Eat the Yellow Snow".

4 September 2016, Sunday

More work on "Mon (Dinosaur) Parc": I double tracked, on the nylon-string, what I recorded earlier on the steel-string.

I felt a bit guilty about giving so much attention to my *Frets of Yore* contribution, thus neglecting the "8" and *Halloween*, so I spent a little time this afternoon practicing all of the etudes and writing performance notes for them, which I plan to include in the portfolio book.

I also worked on "Six Stories Of An Ancient Astronaut", the title of which finally solidified with the music: I have been playing with the idea of "Six Stories" but didn't know "of what". Today the impression of "Ancient Astronauts" floated by (a nebulous reference to "Chinese Astronomy" and the Four Symbols), as the music of "Six..." creates an ethereal – space-like, yet primeval – atmosphere.

6 September 2016, Tuesday

Today, in anticipation of the Taylor GS Mini bass, I recorded a demo of *Halloween* "Ten Hungry (Possible Friendly) Ghosts" using my Fender electric bass, and it sounds fantastic! The octave-down richness of the bass (with all due respect to the 8-string baritone) is what these pieces have been quietly pleading for. I hope I'm not expecting too much from this Taylor bass that I haven't yet seen, heard, or played, but I'm going to make more demos with my current bass so I can be prepared for its arrival.

The one considerable downside of this new development is that I'll have to postpone the recording of *Halloween* from October until...well, until whenever the bass shows up. Quite frankly this is a tremendous risk, as it will easily put the project four months behind schedule. Ugh. Well, this is one of the reasons I gave myself such an extended deadline.

10 September 2016, Saturday

Today I received an impeccably cliché and sentimental store-bought, birthday card from my Mom and Pop – one more appropriate for a pre-teen than a 45-year-old man. Nonetheless, the last sentence perfectly sums up my relationship with my parents: "May you always believe in yourself the way we believe in you."

I am very fortunate and extremely grateful.

11 September 2016, Sunday

Last night R.O.E. gave a superb performance before a large and appreciative crowd; a sold-out show! It was an absolute success and a pleasant way to spend my birthday.

14 September 2016, Wednesday

I played an amazingly good country music gig last night with The Luck Pushers. We drew an excellent crowd that responded enthusiastically to my, what I would normally label "overplaying" – loud, extended, and ostentatious solos. Maybe I don't overplay enough?

15 September 2016, Thursday

Worked on "Four Letters In The Number Four" today. I doubled the length of the piece by repeating it entirely, with the melody performed up an octave and some subtle rhythmic variations added to the accompaniment. This is one of the few pieces in *Halloween* where there is an obvious hierarchy of lead melody, inner voices/accompaniment, and bass: This is probably the reason it comes across as the most song-oriented of the pieces. It's worth mentioning that "Four..." is in the Mixolydian mode, which is charmingly blithe without being saccharine.

16 September 2016, Friday

I presented an EarthQuaker Devices demo last night at Brian's Guitars here in Hamden. It was a good turnout, 20 people in attendance...but it was odd. Afterward I was asked, "Did you have fun?" I replied bluntly, "Not really."

The biggest issue is that it is difficult to tell what the audience wants: To learn about effects in general? To learn more about EarthQuaker Devices? To hear/see me play? For better or worse, I aim to please. I am, after all, there to provide a service – to educate and entertain. Thus I constantly second-guess my role:

❖ Should I play with backing tracks, demoing a distortion, delay, or synth emulator in context?

❖ Should I create real-time loops to play along with?

❖ Should I play a bunch of show-off licks?

❖ Should I talk about tone?

❖ Should I talk about creativity?

❖ Should I talk about myself?

❖ Should I play more, talk less?

❖ Should I know more about the technical and technological side of electronic effects? (I don't know amp bias from compression ratios.)

As a result, I incorporate these approaches en masse. Yet if I catch a glimpse of nonplussed faces in the audience, I assume, "This isn't what they want. You should move on." Consequently, I can't settle in. And then I erroneously blame

111

the audience. Tonight, as frequently happens, they just sat there quietly observing: I should point out that the audience was made up of (and I say this with affection) guitar geeks of all shapes and sizes – tone chasers, shredders, collectors, scrutinizers, etc. – however, in this case their silent contemplations made me self-conscious, rather than self-assured. With few questions and scant feedback, I found it irksome to gauge what they expected. But that shouldn't matter. I should be able to educate and entertain regardless of who sits down or what their manner is.

Solution? I won't do any more demos/clinics unless I have several scheduled consecutively, that way I can develop a routine. I will also reduce the demo time – one hour is more than enough to discuss and play everything – with an additional 15-30 minutes for Q&A.

There were a few positive moments: I created a waggish, real-time, looping, improvised composition using the Spatial Delivery (a quirky envelope filter effect); I revisited my "Being For The Benefit Of Mr. Kite" lesson [see 26 May 2016] and it received spontaneous applause even though (in my mind) I barely played it half-good; and I spoke about my own playing, particularly my obsession with octave displacement and diatonic seconds, these also elicited positive feedback.

With a little distance, and taking both the pros and cons into consideration, it seems like it was a meritorious night. I suppose having an overabundance of topics to talk about isn't such a bad thing.

17 September 2016, Saturday

Just watched the Brian Wilson/Beach Boys bio pic, *Love & Mercy*, and was reminded how much I despise exaggeration, a misrepresentation of facts, and the conferring of value on the wrong aspects of an artist's work.

PET SOUNDS
AND THE MISATTRIBUTION OF VALUE

When in the role of educator, I try to do my best to communicate succinctly on topics that are of importance to me – art, music, objectivity, debunking myths (artistic emperors with no clothes), education, and creativity – without oversimplifying or becoming a reductionist.

I could easily provide an unfavorable, song-by-song analysis – both artistic and historical – of *Pet Sounds* that could withstand the scrutiny of any educated critic, but that's not the point, because I could just as easily explain to you why The Beach Boys singles are peerless. Instead I'm hoping to share my perspective, which I have gained from years of listening to, reading about, studying, playing, and composing music, in order to allow readers to reevaluate their own judgments. I'm also here to validate *unpopular* opinions – contrary judgments that are far too often discouraged by so-called experts.

To me, The Beach Boys' *Pet Sounds* is the musical manifestation of someone trying too hard. You can hear it in every song: Contrived chord progressions and awkward modulations, abrupt and disjointed changes in form and arrangement, and the addition of pretentious and/or novel orchestration when austerity would have served better. Brian Wilson does manage to achieve an elegant cohesion of craft and artistry on "God Only Knows" and "Wouldn't It Be

113

Nice", however; the remaining 11 songs on *Pet Sounds* are uneven and anemic, straining to prove themselves. But I have sympathy for Brian Wilson; he really was all alone. The Beatles had each other, George Martin, Brian Epstein, and many more. If either Lennon or McCartney had composed *and* produced *Sgt. Pepper's Lonely Hearts Club Band* on his own (as Brian Wilson did with *Pet Sounds*) it would have emerged every bit as muddled as *Pet Sounds*. It's important to have friends during the creative process. Heck, it's important to have colleagues, especially ones who can provide constructive criticism and complementary skills.

I am well aware that the Beatles loved and admired *Pet Sounds*, though I've concluded they must have considered it a rough draft: Worthwhile ideas but fundamentally flawed, both compositionally and in production, if well executed technically. The Beatles and George Martin sensed the potential in *Pet Sounds* and used it as a point of reference, though only one of many, when creating *Sgt. Pepper's*.

Is Brian Wilson an artist? Did he write superb songs? You better believe it! "In My Room" (co-written by Gary Usher), "California Girls" and "Good Vibrations" (both co-written by Mike Love) – the list goes on. Even, and especially, "I Get Around" (also co-written by Mike Love) from 1964; the vocal harmonies on that recording are stunning, almost impossible to duplicate, dense and complex yet utterly catchy – Brian at his best. But on *Pet Sounds* he was out of his element...

...I have immeasurable admiration for cartoonist and graphic designers, two art forms that – for better or worse, right or wrong – do not carry the same cache as being a "serious" painter. I want to make it clear that these artists – cartoonists, graphic designers, serious painters – are all equal in my mind, but they each do different things. Brian Wilson is a graphic designer, who, on *Pet Sounds*, tried to reinvent himself as a serious painter. It didn't work. And sadly, he didn't even have to do it. He is one of the superlative 'graphic designers'. I can get serious paintings from someone else. Furthermore I don't yearn to see Vincent Van Gough, Lee Krasner, or Avinash Chandra do graphic design!

But don't take my word for it: I entreat you, dear reader, to listen for yourself, objectively, actively, and with an educated ear and mind – then come to your own conclusions.

And the next time someone tells you *Pet Sounds* is brilliant, ask him/her to name four songs from that record other than "Wouldn't It Be Nice" and "God Only Knows", I promise you they won't be able to, because none of the other songs are catchy or memorable. *Pet Sound* was a good idea but it is not a great record.

20 September 2016, Tuesday

It's 7am and the band Soften the Glare – guitarist Bon Lozaga (who played in a late 1970s incarnation of Pierre Moerlen's Gong, also known as Gong-Expresso), bassist Ryan Martinie (who played in the multi-platinum metal band Mudvayne), and Mitch Hull (Soften the Glare is Mitch's first high-profile band) – are asleep in my house. I set up a show for them tonight, with my band, Emily B.*, opening.

Bon and I have been friends since the mid-1990s. We met on the prog/fusion circuit when I was with Boud Deun and he was playing with his band Gongzilla. I am an avid Gong fan and Bon liked Boud Deun, so we hit it off instantly.

---

* I haven't written about Emily B. because we don't play much (we've only had three gigs prior to tonight) and we haven't recorded any music (though there are some videos online). Emily B. claims to play "art-punk" music, despite the fact that we're just a weird instrumental rock group.

A GONG TANGENT

Regarding Bon's 1990s band Gongzilla, it seems as though anyone who has ever played in any incarnation of Gong (Gong possess a storied and confusing history) formed a band with the word "Gong" in it: Gong, Gong-Expresso, Pierre Moerlen's Gong, Planet Gong, New York Gong, Gongmaison, Mother Gong, and a few more I'm probably forgetting. Thus Bon's Gongzilla.

In case you don't know (and most people don't), the original Gong were a one-of-a-kind, British psychedelic-rock band led by Daevid Allen. In the early 1970s they released a trilogy of albums – *Flying Teapot* (1973), *Angel's Egg* (1973), and *You* (1974). The first two records are good but the nascent concepts therein cohered into a multifaceted, colorful, and rewarding musical journey on *You* – it's brilliant! Gong's music is a combination of Pink Floyd, Frank Zappa, and Dr. Seuss. I'm completely serious, that is exactly what they sound like! The psychedelic sounds of Floyd – vertiginous keyboards, kaleidoscopic effects, and hypnotic drones; the complexity of Zappa – including the intricate unison playing, odd time signatures, angular melodies, and room for improv; as well as the sense of humor and farcical yet unforced, natural but crafted, rhymes of Seuss.

If you reread that description you can see that "songwriting skills" is absent from my list of high-praise and reverential references. The albums in the Gong trilogy don't have songs, they have pieces. I suspect this is the reason they never made it big in the U.S. – most Americans have an appetite for "songs" not "pieces". Regardless, everyone should listen to *You* at least once…no, three times. It can change one's mind regarding the need for songs.

I was overjoyed when, in 1996, Boud Deun got to open for Gong at the Baltimore Museum of Art. We were good – our usual energetic, excitable, overeager selves – but Gong was effortlessly enchanting, almost otherworldly, a true lesson in artistic authenticity. I try to remember the example they set at every show I've played since (though remembering is easier than achieving).

Incidentally, the first time Sting, Stewart Copeland, and Andy Summers – soon to be The Police – performed together in public was on May 28, 1977 during a Gong reunion show (or farewell show, depending on who you ask) with Gong bassist Mike Howlett on vocals, under the moniker Strontium 90.

21 September 2016, Wednesday

A dynamite show last night, all thanks to Soften the Glare. Emily B. was good, though little of our performance is noteworthy, particularly in light of how spectacularly deft Bon, Ryan, and Mitch were. They came on strong and stayed strong for 80 minutes, performing solid rock/fusion instrumentals. Nothing revolutionary genre-wise but tenacious compositions with captivating melodies played by guitar and bass (sometimes one or the other, occasionally in unison, frequently in counterpoint), starts and stops, unison riffs, understated odd meters, and very few solos, all of which I appreciate. Best comparison: a hard rock version of Chick Corea's composed music.

Ryan's bass playing was extremely busy, though at no time in the way, with an uncommon combination of smoothness and ferocity. Bon played a lot of pleasantly jarring diatonic second harmonies: I thought I was the only one obsessed with seconds (which can be tricky to play cleanly because they require a large finger stretch; Bon told me later he tunes his B string down to A, that way he can barre the seconds on the 2nd and 3rd strings – that is a huge and brilliant cheat). And Mitch provided both solid groove and spirited rhythmic counterpoint. The band also has their frequencies harmoniously tuned in so that each player gets sonic space that is complementary, not competitive: that way, even with everyone playing a seemingly overabundance of notes, it was never cluttered. It was an exceedingly commendable performance.

With Soften the Glare as a point of reference, I thought Emily B. sounded like inexperienced punk kids attempting to play fusion (which isn't such a bad thing – frankly that's kind of what I'm going for with that band). Conversely, Soften the Glare was heavy *and* polished. That is tricky to achieve. I'm envious (in the best of ways).

27 September 2016, Tuesday

A great History of Rock class today, comparing and contrasting *Rubber Soul*, *Pet Sounds*, *Freak Out!*, *Revolver*, "Strawberry Fields Forever"/"Penny Lane", *Absolutely Free*, and *Sgt. Pepper's Lonely Hearts Club Band*.

Zappa does not get the credit he deserves for his pioneering work transforming rock music from entertainment into art. Music fans, critics, and educators should focus more on *Freak Out!* than on *Pet Sounds*. *Freak Out!*, though almost as muddled as *Pet Sounds*, is superior in scope musically, conceptually, and socio-politically. And *Absolutely Free*, released a few days before *Sgt. Pepper's Lonely Hearts Club Band*, is a masterpiece of music, satire, and conceptualism, even if the mix is dated. (By the way, Zappa recorded *Absolutely Free* in three days! The Beatles had six months to record *Sgt. Pepper's*, and Brian Wilson spent ten months working on *Pet Sounds*.)

Moved by the dynamic classroom discussion of music and innovation, I came home and formulated a few harmonic and melodic connections for *Halloween* so that "Six...", "Seven...", and "Eight..." , segue into one another. Hmmm...segue is the wrong word. It is correct for the

118

transition from "Seven..." to "Eight...", they end and begin, respectively, on the same note, though they are in different keys. But the movement from "Six..." to "Seven..." is more of an intentional yank, twisting the listener from celestial splendor into erratic instability. I love that contrast.

OCTOBER

2 October 2016, Sunday

Last night I went to see The Fab Faux, a Beatles tribute band made up of top session players and sidemen. The show was great, but it was because the music in and of itself is great. I enjoyed seeing/hearing the band, they did the songs justice, providing a likeness without imitation, and the audience shared in the elation of the music. But it was the entire occasion that was so encouraging. The fact that a sizeable audience (500-1,000) came to listen, really listen, to pop/rock music that is 50 years old, performed by a band with no direct connection to The Beatles; rock and roll embracing the classical music paradigm, hooray!

11 October 2016, Tuesday

You may have noticed that I have written very little in the past two weeks; this is due to several reasons, I've been sick (common cold and headaches); had my kids more than usual, due to school starting, schedule changes, and holidays; accepted three new private guitar students; and been spending a fair amount of time amending the syllabus, as well as prepping audio and video samples for my History of Rock class – which I love and am quite obsessed with.

What you can't see is that I have barely played or practiced in the last two weeks, ever since the show with Soften the Glare.

Reasons for this? Primarily, a complete lack of interest or motivation. This is disappointing as, even though I don't have the Taylor bass, I thought October would be the month to begin working on *Halloween* recordings; but frankly it doesn't surprise me that I'm unmotivated. Setting a goal to work on something by yourself, without a deadline, doesn't make demands on you the way working in a group, with a time limit, does.

Rather than worrying about this, I am adopting a Taoist outlook: The way to do is to be. *Halloween* will be completed in time. Heck, it's been 13 years since I wrote the music, what's another couple of months?

12 October 2016, Wednesday

My kids are in their room listening to *Pustit musíš*, an album by Czech alternative art rock band Dunaj (with Iva Bittová and Pavel Fajt). My son *loves* those songs and my daughter likes them (though she won't listen to them at nighttime, "They're too scary."). They have also been listening to The Descendents, Third Eye Blind, Meghan Trainor, and David Bowie. I'm quite delighted with the range of their tastes. I think setting the stereo up in their room is paying off!

14 October 2016, Friday

I was a bit vexed yesterday when I discovered that Bob Dylan had been awarded the Nobel Prize for Literature. Then I contemplated the word "literature" and recognized that just as music can be *any* sounds (in the right hands), literature can be *any* words – so why not song lyrics? So I took a minute to reflect on all Dylan's poetic and poignant songs: Even as someone who likes Dylan but doesn't consider himself an avid fan, it took me less than thirty seconds to recall a dozen of his brilliant lyrics.

Until I was a teenager I thought "Blowing In The Wind" and "The Times They Are A-Changin'" were traditional folk songs – there was no way one person could have written those songs, they surely must have been developed and appended over decades, if not centuries: They are perhaps the most timeless songs of the 20th century. And those are just two of many exceptional works. Following this train of thought, I summoned up a second dozen, exemplary Dylan lyrics – writing on par, if not superior, to any of the most celebrated poets or writers of any generation. Well done, Bob. Well done, Nobel Prize committee.

15 October 2016, Saturday

This morning I awoke from a rather telling nightmare:

I was touring with a band that was opening for John Mellencamp. I noticed that his group had started using in-ear monitors but they were being powered by a cheap power supply that was causing a high-pitched frequency – almost inaudible but highly annoying – to permeate the sound. The worst part was that they were scarcely saving $100 using this cheaper power supply. I mentioned it to the band's manager and he condescendingly dismissed my concerns, so I said to myself, "Fine. Your problem; not mine."

After this exchange I went onstage to set up my gear and unexpectedly I was told the show was starting and we were on. I wasn't ready. I was futzing with some pedals when the drummer said to the audience, "This is a new song that we haven't figured out yet, so we're going to invite _____ (the sax player in Mellencamp's band – I don't know if Mellencamp has a sax player but in my dream he did) to play it with us." I was shocked and furious. It was my song and I hadn't approved this; I did not want saxophone on it! I turned to the band and yelled, "You can play it without me," and I walked off stage. They started playing anyway and it was awful.

As the band butchered my song, I was getting angrier and angrier while simultaneously enjoying schadenfreude. Backstage, I sat down at a picnic table on which there sat a cake in a pan and next to it a bowl of icing. I grabbed the cake with one hand, torn it out of the pan, and started icing it with the other hand. Then Mellencamp's wife, who, in my dream, was a perfect angel – kind, caring, beautiful, and apparently a close friend of mine – came over and sadly asked, "What's wrong with you?" Suddenly I burst into tears and, with cake and icing all over my hands and in my mouth (it would have been comical except for the fact that it was heartbreaking), said, "I don't know. Everything I try fails. I play country and rock, commercial and outside, but nothing works. What's wrong with me?"

I don't need Freud to figure out this dream. And while I don't feel that way often (and I haven't felt that way in quite some time), this dream confessed a sentiment that I suspect is with me more than I would like to admit. Though I did try to purge these feelings a few years ago…

YOU'RE THE ONLY ONE

This previously unpublished essay from 2009 started as a self-pitying rant (which I fell into after reading the John Zorn curated book Arcana

IV) that fortunately evolved into a, "Get over yourself and get on with the work," bit of catharsis.

If it is not perfectly clear, this piece is ironic. Please keep that in mind, for we all at times feel like we are the "only ones".

You are sitting there, right now, reading this book and thinking, "I'm the only one."

You like this book, you feel as though you've found like-minded people...but...not completely. You're thinking, "Yes, yes, I agree with that guy and that woman...but I don't like their music. They're *too* weird. No, no, that's not it, I like weird; they just play too much noise. Why can't they just write a good, normal 'pop' song? Because they can't! They can't. I can...I'm the only one. I'm the only one doing this. I'm the only one who is trying to bridge the gap between the avant-garde and pop music. I know others have tried, but face it, they don't write good songs!"

And now you're angry. You're angry because no one knows how exceptional you are and you've done everything you can. Everything you know how to do. All the things you're supposed to do.

Twenty years ago you played every gig you could. You created countless hand-made flyers. You drove hours to play 30 minutes and make no money. You even sent out a real mailing list, through the mail! You were okay, not great, but okay. So you listened to new music constantly, looking for ideas, looking for inspiration; challenging both your playing and your composing; studying all the musical giants and learning what they did, and what they did not do. Slowly you got your own thing going and you got better and better. You saw your entire future; you could go one of two ways, Pop Icon, or Avant-Garde Iconoclast. Then it hit you: BOTH! You would do both. You, on the cover of *Time* magazine,

"The Future of Music". This would work.

Five years passed. You put out a few CDs. The first of these on your own label, following in the footsteps of your underground heroes like Sun Ra and Black Flag and remembering that The Beatles also started their own label. Then a "real" label noticed you. A real independent label that is. A small label that you respected. You even liked some of the bands on it, and you thought, "I'm going to make that label famous. I'm going to sell more records for that label than all their previous releases combined." And you did! You sold about 400 CDs.

You were now a voracious music student and that made you happy because you knew you were already accomplished but you were humble enough to know there were new concepts to learn. You read obscure books on contemporary music practices written by 20th-century-nobody-composers who you realized (when you finally heard their music, that you ordered from some record store fanzine from the North of England, and paid twenty-seven dollars just for the shipping) didn't deserve to be famous because their music was unlistenable. Grand ideas, awful execution. But you used their experiments as jumping off points, filling in the missing pieces, like a treasure hunter who found the second half of a severed map. Only *you* know the way.

Five more years pass. You realize you just want to make a living playing music. You don't care about becoming famous (but really you do) you just want to play music, make a living and have respect from your peers, whoever they are, "Because no one, NO ONE," you tell your second wife, "is doing what I'm doing. I'm the fringe of the fringe. I'm too mainstream for the out players; I'm too out for the mainstream. Sure a couple of those guys play in pop bands but they aren't *their* bands, they're sidemen."

You practice insistently, because gigs are few and far between, and you find it difficult to connect with other musicians. This saxophonist only wants to play free improv, this cellist can only play written music, one drummer (who has the best CD collection you've ever seen) actually tells you, "I'm not so good at keeping the beat."

You release another CD, it's good, and it gets more attention than anything you've done so far. You're reviewed by every major music magazine in the country, honestly, no exaggeration; rock zines, indie zines, folk zines, jazz zines, even classical magazines. Why aren't you selling more records? You have a website (this Internet thing is relatively new; you have to go to someone else's house to find out what the Internet is) so you're also on the cutting edge of new technology! Now to turn those magazine reviews into gigs and CD sales.

Five more years. You wish you were resigned to this obscurity. "I'll just be like Robbie Basho or Nick Drake. Famous after I'm dead. Maybe I should just kill myself." Of course you don't mean this because you are not that type at – clinically despondent with genuine depression issues. Maybe that's the reason you aren't a famous musician. You don't have non-musical, emotional issues that drive you, like abusive or dead parents. You tick off the names, "McCartney, dead mom; Lennon, dead mom, absent dad; Clapton, absent dad; Waters, dead dad; Bono, dead mom; Parker, absent dad; Streisand, dead dad; Hendrix, dead mom; Beethoven, abusive father. The list goes on and on. But then, being the levelheaded, logical, *normal* person you are, you think, "This is stupid. There are plenty of illustrious musicians with kind *and* living parents. Besides, I'd rather have my life now, as it is, with my mom and dad alive and encouraging, than have a successful musical career and dead or mean parents."

Five more long, long years. Here you are reading this book. You're still the only one doing what you're doing and you are doing it better than ever. You record. You also write out all of your music, like a real composer, on paper, with notes and staves and archaic Italian instructions. You even transcribe the improvised solos from your first record. You play shows. You sell the odd CD. Sometimes you even get the occasional fan email, out of the blue, "Just found out about you through a friend who bought your CD at a pawnshop. It's awesome. Do you still play?"

Five years from now…and you're still the only one.

16 October 2016, Sunday

It turns out that revisiting the mordant "You're The Only One" was a source of motivation! Today I worked on *Halloween* for the first time in more than a month. It felt fresh and promising. I made some small, rhythmic changes to "Three…", a delicate, slightly abstract, piece that is moderately easy to play, but I need to take care performing the articulations and heeding the dynamic markings. I attempted to record some demos of this piece, but syncing the gossamer-like phrases, which weave in and out and overlap, proved arduous, and the results were sloppy. More practice is required. Still, it was encouraging work.

24 October 2016, Monday

Added two more staves to my score for "Five…". Until now this *Halloween* piece had been a duet but today I doubled each part, even though the piece is already extremely dense ("Too many notes." – "I don't understand. There are just as many notes as are required."). By doubling the parts I make it clear that all those outrageously syncopated, dare I say "arrhythmic", notes are just right! This is a very challenging but tremendously fun piece to play.

26 October 2016, Thursday

Teaching my History of Rock class has become a lot like performing, in the best and worst ways: I do an enormous amount of prep and then when lecture time comes around: Poof! Class is over. I suppose that's a good thing: Who'd want a long-drawn-out class? Nevertheless, there is this post-lecture residue of an extreme desire to teach it again – immediately! A petty complaint to be sure, yet the energy and yearning for more – more time to present and more opportunities to present – persists.

A book is the solution. I'll put all that class material into a book and it will take on a new life; it will actually exist, manifested in physical form. This thought is intensifying as I am submitting a proposal to the university for an honors class I've created, titled "Rock and Roll Goes to Art School: The Parallels Between Rock Music and Contemporary Art*."

27 October 2016, Friday

I completely dismantled "Eleven…" this morning. Then I put it back together again, giving each guitar different notes from the main melody. Now the theme jumps around from instrument to instrument like a game of hot potato! And it's a blast! I was stirred to try this method of redistribution after I made a chart of James Brown's "I Got The Feelin'"** for my History of Rock class. Next time you listen to that tune dig how everyone is playing a different, short, syncopated phrase

---

* This class, now titled: "Rock Becomes Art", was approved a few weeks later. It will commence in the Fall 2017 semester and be co-taught with a professor from the art department.

** Credit where credit is due: By all accounts, in addition to Brown, J.B. bandleader Alfred "Pee Wee" Ellis deserves an acknowledgement for the super funk of this inimitable masterpiece.

– drums; bass; guitars (Jimmy Nolen and Alfonzo Kellum at their understated, almost minimalist, best); I believe even the horns are split up, with different lines for the trumpets/ trombone and saxes; not to mention Brown's vocal – but it all syncs up masterfully. "Eleven…" is my modest homage.

31 October 2016, Monday

It's just a touch ironic that I didn't work on *Halloween* today.

NOVEMBER

3 November 2016, Thursday

MODERN PRIMITIVE MELODIES

"…[Picasso] was possessed of the ambition to mine universes of the mind no one had yet explored."
- Norman Mailer *Portrait of Picasso as a Young Man*

The phrase, "to mine universes of the mind no one had yet explored," [p. 98] struck me hard. I read a lot into it, both for Picasso and myself…

Picasso would come up with an idea/style – blue period, African-influenced, cubist, line drawings, etc. – and exploit it for all its worth, then move on to something new (sometimes revisiting the old).

Now while I would never compare myself to Picasso, I am inspired by his work and methodology. My idea/style is the modern primitive melody: Exploiting an abundance of contrary characteristics (see Appendix II: A Modern Primitive Guitar Primer), yet attempting to make those opposing characteristics as catchy as possible, creating ambiguity and contradiction (my two criteria for Great Art) and allowing my melodies to be:

❖ Dark yet playful

❖ Sophisticated yet naïve

❖ Technically demanding yet sloppy

❖ Haphazard yet exact

Reading that Mailer line about Picasso made all those ideas rush back into my brain, inspiring me to become more diligent and focused on the melodies in *Halloween*.

Halloween is inherently melody driven, but so far I've been focusing on parts – specifically, how all the parts fit together. This attention to arrangement is important, but I if I spend more time playing the melodies – my modern primitive melodies – with élan and a sense of whimsy (as if they were kids' songs or folk melodies, easy on the ear and hummable, even if they're not) then the recordings will be grounded in melody, rather than in the novelty of a guitar string quartet. It's an exciting prospect.

4 November 2016, Friday

I spent most of today following through on yesterday's plan of focusing on melody. In all modesty, the melodies in *Halloween* are something special – I have the Muse to thank for that. I feel there is a genuine cohesion of diverse influences and styles. Some of the melodies, "Four…", "Six…", and "Eight…" are akin to Tchaikovsky's, particularly his ballet themes, airy and vivacious. Conversely, "Two…" and "Five…" are more like Charlie Parker and Dizzy Gillespie's combustible unison lines in "Ko Ko" and "Shaw 'Nuff" (two pieces I've practiced for years but have never been able to pull off). And then there are the recondite, almost amorphous, *Halloween* pieces like "Three…" and "Seven…", with their vague, disjointed themes that are tossed around from guitar to guitar, making them difficult to practice solo. These pieces are influenced more by conceptual ideas, those of John Cage, Meredith Monk, and Pauline Oliveros. It was a jubilant day of music – no expectations, no striving, no recording, just playing.

7 November 2016, Monday

HOW NOT TO BE A MUSIC JOURNALIST

Earning a degree in journalism and owning a CD player does not qualify you to be a music journalist! If you're going to write about music, you should genuinely know something about it and be able to convey those ideas succinctly to an audience. Critics need to stop feeding music fans trivia and gossip, and underestimating their readers' ability to comprehend basic music theory and terminology.

Conversely, many authors who can write intelligently about music theory and practice (as a rule, text or instruction book authors) rely too much on the technical and academic, with little regard for the instinctive, emotional, or social aspects of music. Balance is necessary.

Currently I'm reading a book about the Nick Drake album *Pink Moon*; it's disappointing writing for such worthy subject matter – the book is more about the author's feelings than Drake's music. And yet I can relate…

From the time my kids were born until they were two and four, respectively, *Pink Moon* was the soundtrack for "night-night" time. For a plethora of reasons (that I'd rather not get into) it was a distressingly challenging period in my life. So why on Earth did I listen to such melancholy music, night after night, at such a difficult time? Ironically, it was for sympathetic reasons. We listen to depressing music when we're depressed – as opposed to "happy music", which would seem to be more logically therapeutic – because it helps us feel we're not alone. Misery loves company, even miserable company. Though sadly the way it turned out for Drake – suicide – doesn't validate this conjecture.

In addition to *Pink Moon*, during those early years of parenthood I also searched for solace in John Cage's "In a Landscape" and "Dream", which are the antitheses of what most people know of Cage – his prepared piano works or 4'33" for example – if they know anything. Both "In a

Landscape" and "Dream" were composed in 1948 and are bittersweet, proto-ambient-minimalist pieces far ahead of their time.

Prompted by my reading of the Nick Drake book, for the first time in roughly two years, I am listening to all of this music again. And while it does remind me of those trying times, it does not evoke any sort of post-traumatic stress (the way a crying baby can). If anything, on the verge of tears as I write this, the music feels like a visit from an old friend who provided help beyond measure when I desperately needed it.

Now, contrary to my earlier statements regarding poor music journalism, I realize that what I have just written is about feelings and not about Nick Drake's or John Cage's music. But I can write this because this is an essay in a diary, not a record review. If this were a book about *Pink Moon*, I wouldn't stop there. I would write twice as much on Drake's musical attributes – his penchants for b7s, add4s, and add9s in his melodies; the overtones produced by his idiosyncratic alternate tunings; his distinctive harmonic choices and their colorful extensions – as I just did regarding feelings. I would consider this a necessity, because any examination of music that fails to broach the subject of empirical musical practice will never do more than speculate on the superficial.

9 November 2016, Wednesday

I dare not comment on the election results. It's a can of worms I'm not interested in opening, though I will say this: I voted for Ralph Nader in 2000 and I would do it again.

20 November 2016, Sunday

Today I received the first rough draft artwork mock-up for the *Halloween Baptizm* CD package. It's a beautiful and graceful pencil drawing, highly detailed and full of subtle visual allusion to the music, titles, and overarching themes inherent in *Halloween*. I hired artist Maria Nicklin to do the cover because her style – I say she draws the shadows of things – fits my vision of the *Halloween* aesthetic. Even in black and white the artwork is very inspiring.

21 November 2016, Monday

Today is No Music Day – a day without music, to reflect upon and appreciate music*. I'll be doing my best to observe it. Yesterday I cued up both *Dog Day Afternoon* and *All Quiet On The Western Front*, to play after the title sequences, as both movies are devoid of music excepting the opening credits. I also rescheduled all my Monday lessons for later in the week. And, so as to avoid external forces, apart from going for a walk and picking my kids up from school, I have no plans to leave the house today.

• • •

So far I have done pretty well observing this day of no music. A few shortcomings:

❖ I caught myself singing "The Itchy and Scratchy Show Theme Song" to my son.

❖ My daughter started singing the P.J. Harvey and Bjork version of "(I Can't Get No) Satisfaction" and I couldn't bring myself to stop her.

❖ While doing a math lesson with my son he sang "Ready Or Not, Here I Come" from *Schoolhouse Rock!*

---

* For more information I recommend visiting www.nomusicday.com or the Wikipedia entry for No Music Day.

❖ After a delicious dinner I said to myself, "That was just what I needed," and instantly Elliot Easton's guitar solo from The Cars' song "Just What I Needed" popped into my head (not to mention countless other such train-of-thought musical connections made throughout the day).

• • •

As I near the end of my first No Music Day, I realize today was okay. Instead of playing music, in the morning I read, in the afternoon I played games with my kids, and in the evening I watched *Dog Day Afternoon* (warning: there is a short snippet of music, coming from a transistor radio, in this movie). It almost felt like a day off.

But it was also a little sad: Without exaggeration, today was gloomy because I did not listen to music. For me, this is a good reason to continue the tradition of No Music Day: It is one day a year that is a little bit empty; but also a day to appreciate, all the more, the joy of music-filled days.

24 November 2016, Thursday

No traditional or formal Thanksgiving celebration for me today, though I am thankful for so much. Thanksgiving has never been a big deal in my family – we save up all our holiday cheer (and energy) for Christmas.

Instead, with my kids at their mom's, I took the day off and spent it alone, which has become my tradition. Well not exactly alone. This year I spent it with Captain Beefheart and The Magic Band, listening to songs from *Trout Mask Replica*; watching a couple of Beefheart documentaries; and learning to play "One Red Rose That I Mean". Last year I spent Thanksgiving with Magma.

Inspired by the jagged yet gentle nature of "One Red Rose...", I also spent a couple of hours endeavoring to wheedle and caress ideas out of the "8". Alas, this bore no fruit, but the attempt was worthwhile as it's always good to improve my physical relationship with this rambunctious instrument.

28 November 2016, Monday

I've been engaging in a seemingly random assortment of musical activities the past week. I...

❖ Conducted two interviews to be used as online content for a major music instrument accessory manufacturer (I've signed a non-disclosure agreement so I can't discuss the details).

❖ Transcribed, for guitar, several of the Bach Cello Suites: This endeavor was motivated by reading *The Cello Suites: J. S. Bach, Pablo Casals, and the Search for a Baroque Masterpiece* by Eric Siblin.

❖ Systematically studied all the songs on *Trout Mask Replica*, listening to a few song a day, making lyric charts, gathering together the scant notation that's available online, and reading all the published literature* I have regarding the music.

---

* *Beefheart: Though The Eyes Of Magic* by John French (French, aka Drumbo, was the Magic Band drummer for several albums and is one of the most eccentric and creative drummers ever); *Lunar Notes* by Bill Harkleroad (Harkleroad, aka Zoot Horn Rollo, was one of the many Magic Band guitarists, he played on *Trout Mask Replica* and *Lick My Decals Off, Baby*); and *Captain Beefheart: The Biography* by Mike Barnes. Though I have read all of these books before, it's been illuminating and educational to revisit them, while engaged in this study of Captain Beefheart's music.

❖ Wrote and recorded a "How to Create Solo Guitar Arrangements" lesson for *Premier Guitar* magazine.

❖ Revisited and re-transcribed a few pieces from *The Art of Modern Primitive Guitar* that I have not played for many years. I will be playing a special guitar concert next Saturday and my plan is to play five archetype Modern Primitive Guitar songs and modestly suggest that they could be "an idiom for the future". I am blissfully exhilarated from reexamining these semi-forgotten (how to play them that is) pieces.

29 November 2016, Tuesday

This afternoon my History of Rock students engaged in a debate (I mediated and provided some prompts) regarding skilled vs. unskilled musicians and the aesthetic quality of their corresponding musical creations. This is a topic that frequently comes up in class and commonly rears its problematic head in my everyday life. I'm starting to think the debate, while possibly worthwhile, is ultimately unwinnable.

EXERCISE:
CAN LISTING "WHAT YOU LIKE" HELP YOU UNDERSTAND "WHY YOU LIKE IT?" (DOES IT MATTER?)

List:

❖ Musicians you like, who almost no one could objectively deny are great players (technical), artists, and composers

❖ Musicians you like, who are great technically but are arguably not great composers

❖ Musicians you like, who most people don't like and you completely understand why (too jarring, too edgy, too weird, too difficult, and some are willfully antagonistic)

❖ Musicians you like, who aren't necessarily great technicians but make some of the most visceral and vibrant music

❖ Musicians and composers who are great in all fields, but you don't want to listen to them for extended periods of time (i.e. for more than three pieces in a row); musicians who become tiresome quickly

What do these lists say about you? My lists [for my detailed list please visit www.PresterJohnMusic.com/HallowenBlog] remind me of what guitarist/writer/educator Joe Gore has included in his webpage bio (www.joegore.com/about):

I got my first day job: an editor for *Guitar Player* magazine…A few hundred articles later…my attitude about guitar changed. I'd witnessed musicians without a shred of conventional skill creating sounds that left me breathless. I'd heard players with more ability than most of us could acquire in ten lifetimes disgorge dismal puke.

My knee-jerk reaction to this statement is that Gore is spot on (although his assessment of players with "ability" is more brutal than I would normally put into print). Upon further reflection, my personal lists indicate that there are plenty of players with *and* without ability that leave me breathless. Absent from my lists are plenty of musicians "without a shred of conventional skill" whose music is also dismal.

So what does *that* tell me?

It seems obvious: There is no one way to make music. Musicians without a shred of conventional skill and players with more ability than most of us could acquire in ten lifetimes (and everyone in between) can all succeed and fail, inspire and disappoint, win and lose. And most likely all musicians can be flipsides of these coins at any given time.

Conclusion? I will no longer engage in this debate of skilled verses unskilled musicians, it is untenable.

DECEMBER

25 December 2016, Sunday

A delightful Christmas with my kids, sister, brother-in-law, Mom, and Pop. I am supremely grateful for my family.

JANUARY

1 January 2016, Sunday

As you can see I didn't write much in December (actually I didn't write at all, I added the Christmas note today). Nor did I work on *Halloween* or the etudes. It wasn't that I was unmotivated, merely that December got busy. Between grading exams, school break for my kids, a trip to VA, and the holidays in general…well, I'm sure it's similar to what most people had to deal with.

That said, December was kind to me. And though I didn't work on the big projects, I did play a fair amount of guitar. Nothing serious or demanding, just fun, recreational guitar – noodling and dabbling.

THE UPSIDE OF DABBLING

"The best wrestler is not he who has learned thoroughly all the tricks and twists of the art, which are seldom met with in actual wrestling, but he who has well and carefully trained himself in one or two of them, and watches keenly for an opportunity of practicing them." - Demetrius, quoted by Lucius Annaeus Seneca in *On Benefits: Addressed to Aebutius Liberalis* [p. 196]

"…just dabble with sounds until something starts to happen…" - Brian Eno from *Brian Eno: His Music And The Vertical Color Of Sound* by Eric Tamm [p. 76]

It is challenging and time-consuming to become proficient at any one style of music. Even more so at two. This is why many fiddlers sound extraordinary when playing Irish fiddle tunes (usually in the key of *D*) but are practically useless at other types of music. I'm generalizing of course…except I'm not. Shredder guitarists are accomplished at shredding but inadequate when it comes to performing folk music. Opera stars can move audiences to tears singing the arias of Verdi or Puccini but they're laughable when belting out a Beatles song (trust me, it's been done). There are exceptions: Some musicians are notable for playing country *and* western.

As cynical as I might sound, this one-trick-pony syndrome is an asset, not a fault. It is how one becomes accomplished. So what happens if you value playing genuinely diverse styles of music – say from opera to hip hop, Indian ragas to metal?

The possible downside is that you fall into the trap of becoming, "a jack-of-all-trades, a master of none". But the upside is that you might find yourself in a condition similar to that of my friend Charles O'Meara (aka C.W. Vrtacek, aka Chuck). Chuck once told me, "I can play many different styles well enough, but I'm not great at any of them…except one, I'm an expert – the best actually – when it comes to playing 'Chuck O'Meara Music'!" And he was right! (I highly recommend his recording *Silent Heaven*). And dabbling in different styles is one of the things that has made Chuck's music special.

I always recall Chuck's words when I get down on my playing, and I bear in mind that no one plays better Shawn Persinger guitar than I do!

Postscript: Chuck has also passed on some sage advice that he got from a "hobo jazz guitarist" years ago: "If you stay in touch with the thing that made you want to play guitar in the first place, you'll never go wrong."

RESTAURANT LISTENING MUSIC

Contradictions are a way of life, even in the most upstanding and principled of people. I'm not talking about the contradictions of hypocrisy, but the paradoxical states we all move in and out of throughout our lives. Such are the thoughts that ran through my brain tonight at a local Mexican restaurant.

I was eating with my kids and the piped music in the restaurant was the usual mix of everyday songs from the "classic rock" canon. Then, quite unexpectedly, I heard Miles Davis' recording of "Summertime" from *Porgy and Bess*. What??? One of the greatest theme-and-variations performances ever, in any genre, piped in as background music??? I was nonplussed...

I have spent hours transcribing and practicing this particular Miles Davis recording, trying my best to coax the horn-specific aspects – such as the long, sustained notes that swell in volume and Miles' brass tone in general – out of the guitar; so I know the recording well (I'm emphasizing "recording" because "Summertime" has been recorded countless times: I am speaking specifically of the *Porgy and Bess* studio album with arrangements by Miles and Gil Evans.) Miles' playing on this record is somehow delicate and stalwart, with a devil-may-care attitude that lets one know that Miles doesn't care if you listen or not.

Maybe that's why it could work in a restaurant setting. Eat or listen, or do both, Miles doesn't care. But no, it didn't work. It made me angry. You shouldn't play Miles Davis' "Summertime" as background music. If there is an archetype "listening music", this is it! It was a travesty. And then I thought, "Where else are the people in this restaurant ever going to hear this recording?" (Because I was snobbishly and ignorantly assuming they were all philistines.) So I reversed my haughty, high-handed opinion and I...No I didn't...I wanted to...but I couldn't.

Yes, it's lovely that more people get to listen to Miles Davis' recording of "Summertime". But...but...but...ugh! It's an argument I can't win...and I don't want to make anymore. Go listen to Miles...go eat while you listen...go...go...

In 1993 I was in a Pizza Hut in Bloomsberg, PA. The restaurant had one of those full-length CD jukeboxes and one of the CDs available for play was the soundtrack to the Oliver Stone biopic *The Doors*. Now that CD is filled primarily with what one would expect, The Doors' hits, "Light My Fire", "Roadhouse Blues", etc. But it also contains two unexpected tracks, The Velvet Underground's "Heroin" and a recording of Carl Orff's "O Fortuna" from *Carmina Burana*. Now "Heroin" is hardly family-friendly, chain-restaurant dinner music but the even more subversive piece is "O Fortuna".

If you are unfamiliar with "O Fortuna" let me tell you that it is extremely foreboding music. It has a repetitive bassline that tone paints the "wheel of fortune" (symbolizing the mysterious and capricious nature of fate) and a portentous melody, sung by a menacing choir, that lingers around the two relatively unresolved, and arguably dissonant, notes F and E. "O Fortuna" has been used countless times in movies to evoke feelings of unease and apprehension. In *The Doors*, the piece is used for a scene in which Jim Morrison joins rock journalist Patricia Kennealy in a handfasting ceremony (a neopagan commitment ceremony) that includes a Pagan priestess slicing open the couple's wrist and mingling their blood. In short, "O Fortuna" is unsettling music.

So there I am in the Pizza Hut, in Middle America, on a Friday night, with "O Fortuna" at my fingertips. What to do?

Seconds later the entire restaurant fell silent − like a scene from a horror film with the soon-to-be-victims huddle together, noiselessly waiting to meet their fate. Eventually, someone whispered, with more than a hint of fear, "What the hell is this music?" By then it was too late, "O Fortuna" had climaxed and my good work was done.

24 January 2017, Tuesday

First day back at the University of New Haven, with a new group of eager students who immediately took to singing. (Have I not mentioned? I require my students to sing in class.) The past two semesters students were reluctant, but today, straightaway, almost everyone joined in. Solid tambourine playing too (playing tambourine is also a requirement in my class). A joyful afternoon of music history and song.

25 January 2017, Wednesday

Yesterday's superb History of Rock class got me motivated: This morning it was back to work on *Halloween*! I added some octave displacement* moves to the main melody of "Ten…" and this completely changed the feel in the niftiest of ways, displacing rhythmic accents as much as it does pitches. I also, in optimistic anticipation of the Taylor bass (it should be here in a month), changed the key from B minor to F# minor. I prefer this key as all parts have been transposed down a fourth, thus the bassline is fuller and richer, and the steel-string counterpoint melody has moved to a lower, more comfortable fretboard position.

26 January 2017, Thursday

Advice for my kids (or anyone for that matter): 1) Be kind. 2) Do what you like.

Oddly, as modest and reasonable as those two platitudes sound, they are exceedingly tricky to carry out consistently. The first one is demanding, as it can be emotionally taxing to be kind to everyone, especially to people who are not kind to you. The second one presents its own challenges, namely being able to make a living by doing what you like.

Be Kind. Do What You Like. Perfect in their simplicity and near impossibility.

---

* For more on octave displacement – a technique that, twenty-five years ago, completely changed my approach to guitar – please visit www.weirdguitarlessons.com/no-2-octave-displacement/

27 January 2017, Friday

Just finished reading (for the second time) *45* by Bill Drummond: I can't recall when I first read it; although, I do remember that my sister gave it to me as a Christmas present even though I had no idea who Bill Drummond was or what the book was about. But by the time I read through "From The Shore of Lake Placid", Drummond's account of his time managing Echo and the Bunnymen, I was hooked. Finishing *45* I straightaway read Drummond's *$20,000* and became enthralled with his work.

Bill Drummond is perhaps the most self-aware artist I have ever encountered. He does things that are grand and he does things that are trivial yet he doesn't seem to distinguish between the two. I like this. Bill Drummond just does the work, often seemingly impossible work*. And he conveys the belief that you can too. Consequently, when I finished reading *$20,000*, I composed a piece of music entitled, "Bill Drummond: Silhouette No. 4" and sent it to him for his perusal.

I had already composed three other Silhouettes and...oh my, this is a can of worms...No, not a can of worms: Threads of silkworms. "This is the artistic process," I capitulate with a mistaken sense of post-postmodern self-awareness...

---

* Like talking Tammy Wynette into singing on one of his songs (see "They Called Me Up In Tennessee" in *45*).

SILHOUETTES

I first saw Ray Johnson's semi-abstract cameo "Silhouettes" artworks of his friends and patrons while watching the documentary *How To Draw A Bunny*. I loved the concept of his Silhouettes (watch the film) so much that I co-opted the spirit of them and composed a few musical, semi-abstract cameo "Silhouettes" of *my* friends.

Originally I had a few guidelines:

❖ Silhouettes were to be named after personal friends of mine.

❖ These friends had to be a composers *and* performers.

❖ The pieces were to be short; dense ("dense" as in "lots of information in a small space", not as in "dumb"); and through-composed (continuous, non-sectional, with no improvisation).

Working with these guidelines, I composed three Silhouettes in the winter of 2009, all of which are on the Prester John album *Desire For A Straight Line*.

Come 4 November 2012, as soon as I finished reading *$20,000*, I composed "Silhouette No. 4: Bill Drummond" and contradicted all my previous guidelines:

❖ Bill Drummond is not a personal friend of mine.

❖ Drummond might argue that he is not a composer.

❖ Drummond's namesake piece is long; it isn't dense – it is tuneful and catchy; it is not through-composed – it allows for improvisation.

Thus, as he is a man of paradoxes, it was the perfect Bill Drummond Silhouette.

Forthwith, I emailed Drummond the sheet music even though I didn't know him personally, and he certainly didn't know me at all. He emailed back the following day. In his considerate and gracious "thank you" email he said he was watching and enjoying my video of "Fireman's Drive Inn" while he typed. I was delighted.

I've emailed Drummond roughly five other times in four years and he always responds quickly and kindly. I'm tempted to ask him to write a review of this diary, or of *Halloween*, or maybe provide a book cover quote. But I'd like his write-up to be based on our five short and rather meaningless emails. I don't want him to read the diary or listen to the music.

FEBRUARY

7 February 2017, Tuesday

Tonight I taught a déjà vu lesson: The student was me, twenty-five years ago – a fan of progressive rock but hoping to round out my playing by learning some jazz, even though I wasn't a fan of jazz. A year ago, this new student had taken a couple of lessons with a "strictly jazz" guitarist but found the teacher's snobbish attitude off-putting, with the instructor going so far as to insult the student's taste in music. Undeterred by this inauspicious entree into jazz education, this student heard that I played a little jazz (I'll take on beginner jazz guitarists but I refer advanced players to teachers who are more committed to the idiom) but was also into progressive rock. Tonight, in one lesson, I was able to help this student bridge the gaps between YES and Charlie Parker, Frank Zappa and Miles Davis, Boud Deun and Thelonious Monk. And I was thrilled that he admitted he was willing to study jazz, even though he didn't like most of what he had heard. Boy could I relate!

JAZZ ISSUES

Introduction

I wrote this because all too often I've seen that many non-jazz – rock and popular – music fans feel belittled for "not understanding" jazz, when in fact they just don't like it. There is somehow this cultural intelligentsia ethos that jazz is an indisputably grand American art form and if you "don't get it" you're ignorant *and* disrespectful. I don't know where this point of view comes from (maybe a similar place as any other music snobbery), but I'd like to share an alternative outlook regarding a lack of affection for jazz that is based in sympathy and personal experience.

You see, I have listened to, played, and studied a lot of jazz because there is intrinsic value in it on many levels – personal expression, technical musicianship, its importance in the growth and dissemination of African-American culture in the 20th century, the melding of American and international cultures, the evolution of harmonic, melodic, and rhythmic musical concepts (among others), and much more – but purely pleasurable listening, for me, is rarely one of those levels. I think that might be difficult for non-musicians to understand, but one can love music for more than just the sound of it: Ideas count too.

One last introductory comment: I've been a reductionist in this essay; but that doesn't mean there isn't more than a kernel of truth in what I have written.

The Sound Of Jazz

Jazz, to me, is the music, performances, and compositions of Louis Armstrong, Fletcher Henderson, Duke Ellington, Billie Holiday, Chick Webb, Art Tatum, Charlie Parker, Dizzy Gillespie, Thelonious Monk, Max Roach, Ray Brown, Ella Fitzgerald, Charles Mingus, Miles Davis, John Coltrane, several other pioneers, as well as a thousand other imitators.

And even though there are many subgenres of jazz – Dixieland; vocal performances of "standards" that, in my understanding, would have simply been called "jazz" or even "popular music" back in the 1920s and 30s; Swing, Big Band; Gypsy Jazz; Bebop; Cool Bop; and Free (I'll stop there because others, like post-free jazz and fusion are, to a certain degree, something altogether different) – do you sometimes think that jazz all sounds the same? That's because jazz does sound all the same! That's why it's called "jazz".

The ride cymbal plays "ding da-da ding, da-da ding da-da ding" (or the hi-hat goes "tiis-ta-ta, tiis ta-ta, tiss ta-ta, tiis") the bass goes "boom, boom, boom, boom, ba-da, boom, boom, boom", the piano comps contrived and hackneyed chord changes (Though jazz players will say, with entirely too much infallible authority, "those changes are hip!" No they are not, they're forced and obviously so – comparable to a teenager learning to drive with a stick shift.), and the instrumental soloist performs a melody that is intentionally vague, convoluted, and difficult to follow. That's the sound of jazz!

How To Find Jazz You Like

When I was 18 I listened to and played jazz for at least a year before I found anything I truly enjoyed. Why would I stick with it for that long without enjoying it? Because people I respected told me jazz would make me a better guitar player.

Which, in the long run, it certainly did: Though I wish I had been given better guidance – I could have cut that year down to a month. That year-long search led me to John Coltrane's version of "My Favorite Things". At last, a jazz song I liked. Only it turns out "My Favorite Things" isn't a jazz song, it's a Broadway show tune that Coltrane performed in the jazz style.

Therefore we must differentiate between a "jazz song" and a "jazz performance". A jazz performance is when any song *not* originally conceived as jazz – such as "My Favorite Things" from *The Sound of Music*, "Someday My Prince Will Come" from *Snow White and the Seven Dwarfs*, or the Scorpions "Still Loving You", all performed in the jazz style by John Coltrane, Miles Davis, and Alex Skolnick, respectively – gets played with a ride cymbal going "ding da-da ding, da-da ding da-da ding", the bass going "boom, boom, boom, boom, ba-da, boom, boom, boom", the piano comping conventional (more often than not, diatonic [all in one key]) chord changes, and, thankfully, with the instrumental soloist performing a melody we can follow because we recognize it from its original, catchy, straightforward, pop/rock version. Listening to recordings with this approach is a good way to get into jazz.

The Myth Of Improvisation

Many jazz musicians say jazz is "all about improvisation", however I contest this statement as highly erroneous! Many musicians improvise – J.S. Bach, Ravi Shankar, Bill Monroe, Eric Clapton, Led Zeppelin, King Crimson – and none of them play jazz. And one can play jazz without improvising. Besides which, most jazz musicians don't improvise as much as they claim.

Did you know there are outtakes of John Coltrane's purported "improvisational" masterpiece, "Giant Steps"?

161

Furthermore, those outtakes are almost identical to the sole recording originally released in 1960. That exposes a major myth regarding jazz improvisation – at least as they have been so inextricably linked to "Giant Steps", which, in my opinion, can serve as a microcosm of jazz in general: Coltrane's solo was not improvised!*

I'm not saying "Giant Steps" isn't great, it is great! So is "Countdown", a tune similar to "Giant Steps" (with its "Coltrane Changes") that is also featured on the *Giant Steps* LP. But it wasn't improvised.

(On a slightly different matter: Even better than those legendary masterworks is the little-commented-upon, "Syeeda's Song Flute". "Syeeda's…" is a piece, dare I say "a song", that has more valuable musical content – melody, rhythmic invention, dynamic variation, form/arrangement, and space – in its composed parts [that is to say, non-solo sections] than "Giant Steps" and "Countdown" combined.)

How did this myth of "jazz is all about improvisation" come about? To a certain degree we have to blame it on Charlie Parker and his contemporaries. In the 1940s and '50s, jazz musicians performed on-stage in front of audiences for four to six hours a night, six to seven nights a week, for weeks on end. Then, at some point, they would go into the studio and

---

*Almost every formal definition I have found for "improvisation" reads something like this: "the art or act of creating, composing, performing, executing, or arranging anything without previous preparation." Now, by this definition no professional musician could ever improvise, unless they were playing a new instrument for the very first time, but I certainly don't believe this. I know that there are plenty of situations in which a "prepared" musician can improvise. Nevertheless, the "Giant Steps" outtakes are evidence that Coltrane had rehearsed, not improvised, his solo. I might be nitpicking or making this a semantics issue but to buy wholesale the "Giant Steps" legend (or any musical legend), without scrutinizing it, is to do music and improvisation a disservice.

record several three-minute pieces of music for commercial release. Are we to believe that the one- to two-minute solos Parker and his fellow musicians recorded onto disc had nothing to do with the 24 hours of solos they might have played on-stage the week before?

Jazz Is...

You have to love jazz for what it is. Or you don't. I do. But don't feel embarrassed or guilty for not liking jazz; and don't try looking for "What am I missing?" You're not missing anything. It's not a matter of "either you get it or you don't." It's a matter of "either you like it or you don't."

MARCH

3 March 2017, Friday

The Taylor GS Mini bass arrived on Tuesday and it is absolutely fabulous! It's everything I had hoped for and more. My first impressions: My goodness it plays like…well, honestly, it plays like a "toy". Playing it is effortless and it sounds fantastic – so much fun. Of course "toy" is the wrong word for endorsing such an extraordinary instrument, but between you and me it is the perfect word: What do you want to do with a toy? You want to play with it! And I have – almost non-stop since Tuesday afternoon.

Thus, a new stage of *Halloween* has begun: Today I spent two solid hours working on "Two…", playing and recording the bass, as well as the other three parts. The bass is fat and thick on the recording and all I did was put a microphone in front of it! No offense to the "8", but this bass was the instrument I truly needed.

In addition to the thrill of recording the bass, the **C** section in "Two…" offered its own supply of joy and humor. This section is notable for its use of the whole-tone scale. This scale creates an off-kilter, untethered atmosphere (it's commonly used in background music in television dream sequences, typically played on a harp) that I adore. And while some listeners might perceive this section of music as needlessly complex, dense, and confusing, I prize it as a comic, musical non sequitur. It's funny! Many of the pieces in *Halloween* have a droll, if well disguised, sense of humor.

14 March 2017, Tuesday

Huge snowstorm outside; recording *Halloween* inside. The snow is two-feet deep and not a plow in sight! I couldn't have designed a more perfect day to record. Consequently I worked from sun up to sun down (though I never saw the sun) and completed three master recordings! "One…" and

"The Ninth…" from scratch, plus I finished off "Two…" from a week ago. How's that for procrastination vs. cogitation! It only took one day to record three pieces (not counting the last 11 months I spent thinking about them).

I had a huge revelation while recording "One…", which is the shortest piece in *Halloween* but has also been the trickiest to determine how to perform as a quartet; I think I figured it out! The instruments will enter one at a time – 6-string, bass, 12-string, nylon – with the volume building and the reverb decreasing: Conceptually I am envisioning the listener entering a large, cavernous church, slowly approaching – being drawn in by – the instruments. As soon as the listener is situated, "One…" immediately ends and "Two…" begins on the subsequent downbeat. While all the pieces in *Halloween* have been composed to flow into one another, this segue from "One…" to "Two…" is the most essential.

Hmmm…I have not even mentioned that *Halloween* is a suite. This means the work is an ordered series of instrumentals, in related keys, with related thematic material and motifs. So even though the individual pieces can be played separately and stand on their own, they were composed as a unified whole and are at their best when played/heard straight through. I have not used the word "suite" in the title because I've presumed this was obvious and inherent, especially when one looks at the numerical headings of each title.

19 March 2017, Sunday

This morning I talked with a student who was battling a barrage of tremulous thoughts such as – "My guitar playing is awful. Why am I doing this? What's the point? What's the reward? What am I trying to prove?". I reassured him that these feelings are normal and (in my experience) more periodic than one would desire. Here are a few things I suggest to musicians when these feelings arise:

❖ Take a break.

❖ Play something easy.

❖ Play slower.

❖ Go for a walk.

❖ Remind yourself "This too shall pass."

21 March 2017, Tuesday

Finished reading *A Year With Swollen Appendices* by Brian Eno. Very good. Inspiring to say the least – Eno's book was one of the inspirations for this diary of mine.

Along the way, I kept a "Best of Eno" file, wherein I cut and pasted noteworthy bits of this book into a Word document. Eno's entire text runs for 414 pages yet my "best of" scarcely filled 64 pages, though 64 excellent pages to be sure. Again with the percentages: Does Eno's excellent 26% justify the 74% that's merely fine? You better believe it.

25 March 2017, Saturday

Skilled musicians who are reluctant to "put on a show" are analogous to an educational children's book without pictures! This doesn't require spectacle: The visual can serve the music!

Smarty Pants (that's me) is formulating a multi-media performance concept for *Halloween* – music, spoken-word, and visuals. A mix of…I was going to reference Larry Coryell, Spaulding Gray, and *La Jetée*, but evoking the name "Laurie Anderson" sums it up!

APRIL

11 April 2017, Tuesday

Two weeks ago, I started reading both *The Art of String Quartet Playing* by M.D. Herter Norton and *The Art of Quartet Playing: The Guarneri Quartet In Conversation with David Blum* by David Blum, as I had hoped they might be helpful guiding my performance and recording of *Halloween*. They indubitably are.

Originally I had thought that the idea of me playing all four parts of a guitar quartet was counterintuitive: Shouldn't each part ring out with its own personality? But the more I read the aforementioned books, the more I understood that, yes, each part should possess its own voice – its own artistic temperament – but ultimately the four players need to, in the words of David Blum, "…bring those temperaments together to forge a unity…" [p. 3] What better way to do this than to play all four parts myself?

Besides the concept of unity, these books have proven valuable in many other ways: Providing useful advice on everything from articulation, dynamics, and vibrato to interpretation, seating position (which I have translated into mixing position), and the need to sometimes "…sacrifice ease for character." [p. 63] This last aspect, as the Guarneri Quartet's first violinist Arnold Steinhardt put it, has proven a truism throughout *Halloween* – particularly on the 12-string, which has required several, unintuitive, awkward fingerings to be employed (sacrificing ease) so as to keep certain phrases on either the octave or unison strings (for character).

I recommend both of these books to anyone who plays in an ensemble – this applies to rock bands as much as it does string quartets – as there is much food for thought for anyone in the role of team player…even for a team of one!

170

14 April 2017, Friday

Today I was offered the opportunity to compose approximately 30 minutes of background music for a lecture produced by The Great Courses*. This comes at an inopportune time as I need to focus on *Halloween*, but the chance seems too good to pass up. I have the weekend to mull it over.

15 April 2017, Saturday

Spent a good six hours – yes six hours! – recording "Ten...", it's getting there, though my erratic mood swings along the way are a bit demoralizing. Jeez, do I have to write about the mood swings? I suppose I should clarify at least a little bit. I'm reluctant because I've always assumed that every artist, during some process of the work, moves though certain mental variations of volatile waxing and waning: One minute, shouting with joy, "I'm a genius! The world will be so grateful for my contributions to mankind!" The next, screaming in frustration, "I'm an idiot! This is worthless! I should just quit."

But I don't quit. "This too shall pass." Although I also know, "This too shall return." Thank goodness it only happens when I'm recording.

16 April 2017, Sunday

I spent most of this Easter Sunday recording "Four..." and "Midnight". Mood swings aplenty but good work was accomplished.

---

* The Great Courses is a series of college-level audio and video lectures produced by The Teaching Company.

There are these wonderful rests in the bassline of "Four…" – yes, rests – that I absolutely adore: Unexpected, and almost unnoticed (the burden of the bassist), silences that throw the melody into stark relief. Like a soft, sharp intake of breath. So fun to "not" play.

17 April 2017, Monday

After careful consideration I decided to turn down the composition job offered by The Great Courses. It wasn't feasible for me compose *and* record 30 minutes of music by their deadline. Instead, I offered my services as the music supervisor: This entails choosing appropriate background music from a library service and requires a much shorter time commitment. They accepted.

18 April 2017, Tuesday

More work accomplished (recording and revising) on "Six…". This piece is truly stunning. The melody bounces back and forth between the 6-string and nylon the first time through, which makes it tricky to follow, but then the 12-string takes over completely on the repeat and the theme sparkles into lucidity. The key ambiguity also provides some mystery, as the piece vacillates between *C#* Dorian or *E* Lydian. I'm thrilled with how this piece is coming together.

22 April 2017, Saturday

Today is the one-year anniversary of this diary. One thing I've come to realize – this book is my ego; *Halloween Baptizm* is my id.

THE *HALLOWEEN* PROCESS

For the past two weeks I have been energetically recording and revising the *Halloween* pieces. There is a tremendous irony in the fact that last year I wrote so much about music when I wasn't playing or recording it, and now, when I'm playing and recording so much music, that *should* be documented, I'm barely commenting on it! I suppose I can only give my attention to any one procedure at a time.

The two key points I should be detailing are the recording process (How does one man record a guitar string quartet by himself?) and how I have to constantly revise for a myriad of musical considerations – harmonies, dynamics, articulations, fingerings, etc. – once I've completed the first recorded demos and find compositional adjustment necessary. Let's see if I can summarize:

❖ The music has been notated in Finale: I've practiced it quite a bit.

❖ I save the Finale notation files as MIDI files and import them into Logic; Logic can then provide me with a computer-generated performance of the notation, which I can use as a backing track to play along with.

❖ I play along with the MIDI, one part at a time, while recording what I consider to be my first draft demo of any given part.

❖ After all four parts have been recorded I start revising for musical considerations such as rhythms, dynamics, articulation, harmonies, etc.

❖ After revisions, I re-record each part, this time playing along with my first draft audio, minus the part I am re-recording.

❖ Now I have a second draft of audio. Hopefully the performance is coming together. If need be (usually there is a need) I record parts a third time.

❖ Take a break. Let the piece marinate. Listen in 24 hours. If it needs a fourth draft I'll start again.

This process takes about…hmmm…I haven't been keeping track. An estimate: I have recorded seven pieces; I have been recording and mixing for approximately 40 hours; and I have about ten minutes worth of music finished! That's four hours a minute! Goodness, that seems slow. But let's not forget, I'm recording four different parts for each piece. So even though all seven pieces only add up to ten minutes, each piece has four parts, so that's 40 minutes worth of music I have actually recorded. That little logistical fact makes me feel better. Only six more pieces to go.

24 April 2017, Monday

Today I spent a lot of time trying to reconcile all the weirdness of "Seven…" by making it a bit more "guitaristic". I don't mean to say I mind the weirdness, but this is by far the oddest and most challenging piece (playing- and listening-wise) in *Halloween*. I thought that adding a few guitar-centric articulations – large interval slides, natural harmonics, and bends – might make this piece more accessible to guitarists in general. I'm not sure it did – in fact, it might have made it even weirder – but I like the result of today's work.

MAY

9 May 2017, Monday

Updated, full-color artwork has arrived from Maria Nicklin and it is marvelous! The art is nuanced, symbolic, and just plain beautiful. The water in particular – I can hear the waves splashing against the shore. I am so thrilled that the music and the art are complementing each other so bewitchingly.

13 May 2017, Friday

Until recently, *Halloween* has been a "top secret" project. Only a few close friends were aware of the work I have been engaged in for the past year. But as the project nears completion, I'm giddy with anticipation and I have been mentioning *Halloween* to more people, particularly my private guitar students. I must admit, once I get talking about *Halloween*, my enthusiasm is difficult to contain. And, as much as I'd like the final package of music, art, and a multitude of allusions to be surprising, I find myself revealing and rambling on about compositional approaches, showing the artwork, and even playing samples. Thankfully, many of my students seem keenly interested and inspired by my uninhibited loquaciousness, prompting the same question time and again, "Where do you get all these ideas?"

SOURCES OF INSPIRATION

Although I occasionally struggle with motivation, inspiration has never been an issue for me. That's because in many ways I am an artistic scribe and puzzler. The Muse gives me ideas on a regular basis but I have to figure them out. That's where the creativity comes into play. I have to write the ideas down; fit them together; try this piece here – no, that doesn't work – how about this? – no, that doesn't work either – what if I try... – perfect!

Some puzzles are easier than others. For example: "First Date" (my funny-when-you-hear-and-see-it-live, scary-when-you-listen-to-it-alone, "stalker" song) arrived fully formed; it only took me 20 minutes to write it down. The same is true for "Sandpaper Polish", "Wenders", "You Tell A Lie", and many others songs of mine.

On the other hand, some puzzles require patience and persistence: The first verse of "Foolish" traveled around the world with me for three months (from Darjeeling, India to St. Petersburg, Russia) before I figured out verses two and three, the bridge, and the vocal arrangement (which David Miller helped me with four years later); "Saints" was a hastily scribbled, four-note bassline with a rudimentary, step-wise melody that lingered in a guitar tab notebook before I revisited it weeks later, added some octave displacement and went on to record three different versions of it; and *Halloween* has patiently waited for 14 years to be completed.

Then there is a combination of the two processes: The first two verses of "Start Again" and "Domesticated" and two-thirds of "Leaving Jerusalem" came in a flash, taking about as long to compose as they are to perform; but I had to contemplate their endings for a few weeks before I was able to finish them.

And there's one other ingenious process (which I learned from J.S. Bach) that I've used on "Betray Your Country", "Sherman Hairpin", and "Fare Tredici" – you compose the first half of the song and then play it backwards.

On those occasions when I don't feel creatively inspired, I simply play and study someone else's music: This is usually enough to stimulate me – productively if not artistically. The key is to learn from as many different styles and instruments as possible.

I have spent hours transcribing music by ear (I'm not very good at it but I get close enough*) and filling notebooks with everything from melodies by Tchaikovsky, Carol King, and Stevie Wonder to Irish jigs, African kora music, and Chinese *sizhu yinyue* ("silk and bamboo music"), not to mention solos by Ella Fitzgerald (scat), Fred Wesley (trombone), and Angus Young (guitar – I can still play every one of Angus' solos from *High Voltage* to *Back and Black*), and countless others.

In a nutshell, my tips for staying inspired: Listen. Play. Puzzle. Play. Listen some more.

27 May 2017, Saturday

At 8am, I started recording the finale of *Halloween*, "Fare Tredici" (which literally translates as "To Do 13" and in Italian means to "Hit the Jackpot", or "To Have Big Luck"). By 7pm I was done. It's fantastic! I am overjoyed with the results. It was a massive undertaking as "Fare Tredici" is the longest *Halloween* piece, consisting of 12 discrete sections, performed with five different tempos.

"Fare Tredici" is also an overture (of sorts) in reverse, by which I mean:

❖ This overture is at the end of *Halloween*, not the beginning.

---

* Years ago, I was reassured that "close enough" was valid when I read an interview with Steve Howe (guitarist for YES) in an old *Guitar Player* magazine (April 1973) in which he said, "I've always found it difficult to sit down and work licks of records. But I didn't get too discouraged, because it was almost like the tune. In a way [this encouraged] the style of not quite getting it right and then adding a certain amount of one's own personality to it." [p. 25]

❖ Each section of the overture is based on a theme from pieces "One…" through "Midnight", running in reverse order of their original appearance: Accordingly, section **A1** is based on "Midnight", section **B2** is based on "Eleven…", etc.

❖ I took what I perceived as the main theme of each piece (or my favorite section) and played them backwards, or rather I recomposed them, using the backwards theme as a starting point. Not all themes worked perfectly backwards, so pitches, rhythms, arrangements, etc. were modified by artistic license. Additionally, parts were swapped: If, in the original piece, the 6-string played the melody and the bass played a bassline, then in the overture they traded roles.

Today's recording of "Fare Tredici" gets added to at least 16 hours I have spent composing these three minutes-twenty-six seconds worth of music (thirteen minutes-eighteen-seconds worth, if you count all four parts). 25 hours, whew.

28 May 2017, Sunday

With the recording of "Fare Tredici" completed, I'd like to say there is light at the end of the *Halloween* tunnel, but anyone who has ever released a record (or book, movie, etc.) knows that the release is just the beginning. There is so much more to do, namely promotion, promotion, promotion.

To a certain degree I am in an advantageous position, as the commission I was given last year will cover most of the production costs of *Halloween*. However, I still need to raise enough money to cover initial manufacturing and promotional expenses, thus I plan to launch a Kickstarter campaign next month to initiate pre-orders.

I ran a Kickstarter campaign in 2014 with illustrator Tom Shultz for our children's book *I'm An Alligator. I'm a Crocodile.* That campaign was a huge success – we exceeded our goal in less than a week. My hope is that *Halloween* will find a similarly receptive, if niche, audience. I am well aware of the pitfalls of releasing a physical CD in the 21st century but I have come to view *Halloween* as a multi-media project (music, books, art), with varied audience potential.

30 May 2017, Tuesday

Spent most of the day working on "Performance and Composition Notes" for the *Halloween Baptizm* notation portfolio book. I don't think I've mentioned this since April 2016: In addition to this diary, there is an accompanying, 100-plus page book that includes the scores for all the *Halloween* pieces, in standard notation and guitar tab*. That portfolio also includes commentary geared specifically towards musicians with a more academic – music theory-based – perspective than the conversational tone of this diary.

---

* In *The 50 Greatest Guitar Books* I included a short entry on the importance of guitar tablature as a highly beneficial supplement to standard notation. It is my belief that if more pieces of classical music – particularly ensemble compositions – were available to guitarists with tablature, we would see an increased understanding of classical composition practices and performances techniques, which are lacking in most guitarists (including myself). Standard notation and guitar tablature are analogous to written language, in fact they are written languages! But most guitarists are not fluent in both. Guitar tablature provides a translation for those of us who struggle when reading standard notation.

JUNE

14 June 2017, Thursday

I have made a serious decision regarding the release of *Halloween Baptizm*. Though the work is short, 22 minutes long, I believe it stands on its own and should be released by itself as an E.P., without the 8-string baritone etudes.

If I include the etudes I feel they would distract or be considered filler, which they most certainly are not, but they are not complementary to *Halloween*. Any scheme – logistic, artistic, or economic – that could diminish the impact of either *Halloween* or the etudes is not one I want to be part of.

I have informed my patrons of this development and they are one hundred percent supportive, going so far as to say, "As creator, you have complete control on where the project goes." I am grateful and humbled by their support and confidence in my work. I will be sending my patrons recordings, notation, and performance notes of, and for, the 8-string baritone etudes, but the commercial release of those pieces will have to wait.

18 June 2017, Sunday

I'm trying to tie all this *Halloween* work together:

❖ *Halloween Baptizm* will be released as a 22-minute EP.

❖ The 8-string baritone etudes will not be included or released at this time.

❖ I am planning to launch a Kickstarter campaign to raise money for the final production costs – music mastering, pressing of CDs, printing of books.

❖ I will stop writing in this diary the day after the Kickstarter campaign has finished.

JULY

1 July 2017, Saturday

A few years ago Gonzalo Fuentes [see 2 September 2016] offered to provide me with album artwork if I ever needed it. Today I asked him if, rather than album art, he would like to contribute some drawings to this diary. He responded with alacrity, thus I am elated: More art!

Fuentes drawings and paintings are a whimsical combination of Art Brut and, according to his bio, Musique Concrete techniques*. I am particularly fond of his mischievous black and white characters (a multitude of them are featured on the *Frets of Yore* cover), so I have asked him to create a dozen of those figures to accompany some of the titled entries in this book. If they turn out half as good as the *Frets of Yore* art I'll be overjoyed.

6 July 2017, Friday

Goodness gracious, Gonzalo Fuentes just sent me two drawings he's completed for this diary. I'm speechless! There are more figures and symbolism in these two drawings than I had expected to get from him overall. I have no words other than "Thank you Gonzalo!"

7 July 2017, Saturday

Just finished the final mixes for *Halloween*. I am very happy.

On Monday I'll send the mixes to Greg Reierson at Rare Form Mastering. Greg is the mastering engineer I have used for my last two recordings; he does excellent work, though what he does and how he does it (he makes the record sound even better) is a bit of a mystery to me.

---

* For more information and art please visit www.guerrillagraphics.cl

11 July 2017, Tuesday

Today I launched a Kickstarter campaign to attempt to raise at least $4,000 in order to pay for CD duplication, book printing, and promotion costs. I wasn't crazy about doing this, I'm a reluctant self-promoter (Really? Aren't you just about to publish a 200-page dairy?), but I understand the necessity. I need to remember, I am not collecting funds; I am offering, in the erudite (Or are they confusing?) words of Chris Cutler, "goods using the new means of creation and production to embody aesthetic and affective 'meanings', as use-value, to communicate directly with a mass public."* Yeah, that's what I'm doing.

26 July 2017, Wednesday

The Kickstarter campaign ended today, it was successful. I raised $4,030 in two weeks, $30 over my goal.

And with that, this phase of *Halloween* is complete. It feels outrageously anti-climatic. All the work I put in during the last year, the last six months in particular, seems so long ago. I'm looking forward to getting though the manufacturing and promotion process and playing some *Halloween* gigs, I feel prepared for that. And as there are some that say luck is what happens when preparation meets opportunity, I say to myself *"Fare tredici."*

---

* Cutler, Chris "'Progressive' Music, 'Progressive' Politics?" *File Under Popular* [p. 159]

APPENDICES

APPENDIX I: THE 8-STRING BARITONE

There can be much confusion caused by the extra strings and the tuning of the 8-string baritone. The "8" has the same basic layout and outward-design as a normal 6-string guitar except for two crucial features:

What would be the two middle strings of a normal 6-string guitar (the fourth, *D*, and third, *G*, strings) are, on the "8", each supplemented with strings an octave higher, like a 12-string, hence the "8" strings. So, even though there are eight strings on the "8", it is valid to refer to the strings as (high to low) first string, second string, third string, etc.

The "8" is also tuned a fourth lower than a standard guitar, thus the tuning (low to high) *E A D G B E* on a 6-string, sounds *B E A D G# E* on the "8" (if one strums an *E* chord shape on the "8" one will hear a *B* chord). For the sake of ease, if not fact, I refer to the string pitches, chords names, etc. as if the "8" was in standard tuning.

In closing, the wording of this appendix, which took an excruciatingly long time to formulate, can serve as a microcosm of just how odd and obtuse the "8" is. For more, and a different take, on the "8" see Jim Kirlin's article "Range Rover" in the Fall 2009 issue of Taylor Guitar's *Wood&Steel* [p. 22].

APPENDIX II: A MODERN PRIMITIVE GUITAR PRIMER

Disclaimer: I would be the first to admit that this primer is a little stiff and a bit longwinded (if you've ever been to one of my performances you know I can be loquacious but *never* uptight), but I wanted to fully convey what I believe Modern Primitive Guitar is all about. That said, this is no manifesto but rather a snapshot of a particular time and personal interest.

What Is Modern Primitive Guitar?

Modern Primitive Guitar is a world of musical paradoxes:

❖ Dark yet playful

❖ Sophisticated yet naïve

❖ Technically demanding yet sloppy

❖ Haphazard yet exact

It is a style of guitar music that is the aural equivalent of the visual Modern Primitive art form explored and developed by such painters as Jean DuBuffet, Joan Miro, Pablo Picasso, William Henry Johnson, Paul Klee, Asger Jorn, Karl Appel, and Jean-Michel Basquiat. All of these artists were highly skilled yet worked with a more visceral approach, technique, and vision. The same attitude and ideas are found in the Modern Primitive Guitar style.

Sonically, Modern Primitive Guitar combines the radical musical styles of experimental/fringe musicians such as Eugene Chadbourne, Fred Frith, and John Zorn with the more traditional leanings of guitarists such as Leo Kottke,

Michael Hedges, and Larry Coryell. The vocabulary and form found in the music of such "concert works" composers as Anton Webern, Leonard Bernstein, and Astor Piazolla also play a role in the Modern Primitive Guitar sound.

The term Modern Primitive Guitar is derived from both the Modern Primitive visual arts (also known as Outsider Art and L'Art Brute) and as a permutation of the term "American Primitive Guitar" coined by musician John Fahey.

What Are The Key Elements Of Modern Primitive Guitar?

As the name implies, a major element of the Modern Primitive Guitar style is contradiction; the mixing of genres and themes that seem radically dissimilar yet coexist happily by building off each other's differences. Prime examples of this are the musical paradoxes mentioned earlier. Other characteristics that are not necessarily contradictory, and certainly are not exclusive to any one genre, include:

❖ Dissonance

❖ Nontraditional song structure

❖ Brevity

❖ Rhythmic invention

❖ Large interval leaps (octave displacement)

❖ Angular melodies

❖ Odd meters

❖ Aggressiveness

❖ Abrupt changes in tempo, key or meter

190

❖ Sound effects using extended technique, i.e.:

- o Using the guitar as a percussive instrument

- o Playing notes behind the nut

- o Bending the headstock and guitar neck

- o Scraping the strings in a coarse manner

Ultimately there are no hard and fast rules for Modern Primitive Guitar, only elements of style. I am not interested in limiting myself (or anyone else) to these few components. Nevertheless, these are the main ingredients that create the foundation for the Modern Primitive Guitar sound.

Interestingly enough, when presented with a workshop on Modern Primitive Guitar, different audiences can have different ideas of what "modern" and "primitive" mean. What is new and unusual in one genre of music is often viewed as standard repertoire in another and vice versa. When giving a talk and demonstration at an academic based composers conference in Washington D.C. audience members found the idea of extended technique to be conventional in the realm of "concert" music: whereas in the world of the mainstream music listener, extended technique is often a new and eye/ear opening concept. Additionally, what most 20th century composers consider to be standard "modern" musical vocabulary i.e. the use of dissonance and pantonality (or atonality as it is more commonly known) or extreme arrhythmic syncopation, is still very foreign, shocking and "primitive" sounding to commercial audiences. It is the unification of these two distinct worlds of music I am interested in.

Who Plays/Composes Modern Primitive Guitar?

As far as I know, I am the only musician or composer to have used this term to distinguish a style of music. But I would not dare to claim I am the only person playing the guitar in this manner. There are far too many guitarists on the planet for such a statement to be valid. In my research I have found other guitarists who have similar leanings but, to my knowledge, have not produced an extended body of work or given it a classification. Composers I consider influences of this genre include Janet Feder, Marc Ribot, and Don Van Vliet (aka Captain Beefheart), as well as all of the aforementioned artists.

I must mention that the exceptional Cuneiform Records compilation CD *156 Strings* (which includes one of my recordings) features several guitarists working in a similar vein, though most with strictly experimental slants.

If anyone reading this knows of other guitarists or composers working in a comparable style I would love to learn about them – I have no interest in flag planting.

Appendix III: *HALLOWEEN BAPTIZM* ALLUSIONS AND EASTER EGGS*

What Beatles fan isn't at least a little bit entertained by searching for "clues" from the "Paul is Dead" myth? Such as the outlandish, if feasible, interpretation that the cover of *Abbey Road* represents a funeral procession: With Lennon, in white, as the angel; Ringo, in black, as the undertaker or priest; Harrison, in denim, as the gravedigger; and McCartney, barefoot and out of step with the others, as the deceased. Or how about hunting for the equally subtle, though absolutely intentional, theme of the four elements – earth, air, fire, and water – in the packaging of Pink Floyd's *Wish You Were Here*. And then there's the lesser-celebrated Pixies *Bossanova* album art, with inset pictures alluding to song titles, not to mention the globe that features the mythical continent of Lemuria!

Perhaps you can tell I'm passionate when it comes to allusions, secret messages, and inside jokes. Accordingly, once the first few emerged in *Halloween* (I didn't plan them, they simply materialized) I couldn't resist adding as many as possible. Thus, every piece in *Halloween* has at least two ("Six...") has as many as five) and there might be more (Easter eggs even I haven't found).

---

* The contemporary use of the term "Easter Egg" has come to describe an intentional inside joke, a hidden message, or a secret feature of a video game, DVD, or any work of art. The term suggests the gleeful nature of a traditional Easter egg hunt.

Spoiler alert! Read no further if you like to find Easter eggs on your own.

I have no delusions regarding the niche audience *Halloween* is likely to attract, so at the risk of assuming that few are going to look for the abundance of allusions and Easter eggs in the music, titles, and artwork of *Halloween Baptizm*, I offer a summary.

One Zero: Periodic Orbits From Chaos To Order And Back

❖ The opening musical interval is a unison, a 1:1 ratio, referencing the title.

❖ The pitches in the melody (though not all of the rhythms) create a musical palindrome; they are the same forward and backward.

❖ This melody also concludes "Fare Tredici", bookending *Halloween*: From chaos to order and back, or vice versa.

❖ The water in the album art appears to be surrounding an island: In fact the image is a curved view of a river running east to west (or vice versa), with sunrise and sunset. The rising and setting suns represent periodic orbits. The ambiguity of direction is an allusion to the musical palindrome.

Two Is The First Sophie Germain Prime

❖ The opening musical interval is a descending major second, referencing the title.

❖ In a certain way, "One Zero" acts as an introduction (and, as we'll see, finale) to *Halloween*. Thus "Two..."

194

is the first fully developed, or rather "traditional", piece in *Halloween*.

Three Hundred Years Of A Hypothetical Moon

❖ In simplest terms, this piece is in the third mode of the *D* major scale, *F#* Phrygian, referencing the title.

❖ The moon in the album art may or may not be hypothetical.

Four Letters In The Number Four

❖ The opening harmonic interval between the bass and the 6-string (which carries the melody throughout) is a fourth, referencing the title.

❖ There are four bodies in the album art (or are there two seen from different angles?), representing the guitar quartet.

Five Planets Visible With The Naked Eye

❖ The interval known as a tritone, also known as a ♭5, is rampant throughout "Five...", referencing the title.

❖ The five planets visible with the naked eye can be seen in the album art.

Six Stories Of An Ancient Astronaut

❖ The opening harmonic interval between the 6-string and nylon is a major sixth, referencing the title.

❖ The title references the Greek god Apollo, who was/is the god of the sun and the muse of music (among other things).

- The original American space program is named after Apollo.

- The sun in the album art represents the ancient astronaut.

- The title also hazily alludes to the Four Symbols of Chinese Astronomy, named by ancient Chinese astronomers.

Seven, The Magic Number (Plus Or Minus Two)

- "Seven…" is in the key of B Locrian, the seventh mode of the C major scale, referencing the title.

- The opening harmonies, G and A followed by B and C, are, respectively, a minor seventh and major seventh, referencing the title.

- The title refers to "The Magical Number Seven, Plus or Minus Two: Some Limits on Our Capacity for Processing Information", a 1956 paper by cognitive psychologist George A. Miller on the number of objects the average human can hold in working memory.

Eight Queens On An Imaginary Chess Board

- The bass and nylon melodies are performed in two different octaves: Numerically speaking the intervallic distance of an octave is an eighth (though it is never called an eighth – the term comes from the Latin: *octavus*: eighth), referencing the title.

- The "Eight Queens" puzzle refers to the problem of placing eight queens on an 8x8 chessboard so that no two queens threaten each other.

The Ninth Day Of The Ninth Month

❖ The interval between the second bass note (which is the key root note *G*) and the first melody note, *A*, is the distance of a ninth, referencing the title.

❖ The Double Ninth Festival is a traditional Chinese holiday (also celebrated in other Asian countries), observed on the ninth day of the ninth month in the Chinese calendar. It is believed that this festival may have originated to drive away danger, but, like Halloween, over time it became a day of celebration.

❖ The poem "Double Ninth, Remembering my Shandong Brothers" by Wang Wei (699–759) is well-known throughout China. "The Ninth…" does its best to humbly reflect this solemnity.

"Double Ninth, Remembering my Shandong Brothers"
by Wang Wei (699–759)

As a lonely stranger in a foreign land,
At every holiday my homesickness increases.
Far away, I know my brothers have reached the peak;
They are wearing the *zhuyu*, but one is not present.

Ten Hungry (Possibly Friendly) Ghosts

❖ The opening musical interval between the **A** section bass and 12-string, as well as the **B** section melody, is the distance of a tenth, referencing the title.

❖ The Hungry Ghost Festival is a traditional celebration held in several Asian countries. According to tradition, during this time, the gates of the underworld are opened and hungry ghosts are free to roam the earth in search of food and entertainment.

197

Eleven Days Disappeared

❖ The opening interval between the nylon and the 12-string is the distance of an eleventh, referencing the title.

❖ Eleven is the first *repdigit*, a natural number composed of repeated instances of the same digit; thus there is quite a bit of repetition in "Eleven…"

❖ In 1752, England adopted the Gregorian calendar, which had already been in use in Europe for 170 years. In order to align the dates, England had to lose 11 days, thus September 3 through September 13 were "made to disappear".

Midnight

❖ All 12 chromatic notes are present in the piece, referencing the title.

❖ The album art represents a 24-hour day; the middle of the middle panel is midnight.

❖ Midnight and Halloween enjoy a special relationship, as in many superstitions and folk beliefs, the witching hour is 12:00am, a time when supernatural creatures are thought to appear and to be at their most powerful. This believe in paranormal activity is reflected in the dark and (seemingly) chaotic music of "Midnight".

Fare Tredici: A Blessing For Korzybski's Map
(From Order To Chaos And Back)

❖ *Fare Tredici* can be translated as "To Do 13", which in Italian means to "To hit the Jackpot", or "To Have Big Luck".

❖ The subtitle, "Korzybski's Map (From Order To Chaos And Back)" is based on Alfred Korzybski's maxim, "The map is not the territory." Korzybski (1879 – 1950) posited that no one can obtain direct access to reality, because reality is limited by both the human nervous system and the languages humans have developed.

❖ Themes from the previous 12 pieces make up this thirteenth piece.

❖ "Fare Tredici" ends with the melody from "One Zero", bookending *Halloween*, from order to chaos and back.

❖ The owl in the album art, like the phrase *fare tredici*, represents good luck.

❖ The album art, in addition to being a landscape, is a map.

❖ The rising and setting sun represents periodic orbits.

Additional Allusions

❖ The owl plays a symbolic role in almost every cultural mythology, from a blessing to a bad omen. For me the owl represents wisdom and good fortune, though I also like the idea that not everyone agrees with this point of view. Therefore the various incarnations of the owl on the album cover, book, and poster play a significant role in the overarching theme of superstition inherent in *Halloween*.

❖ The chicken on the album cover is named "Halloween", after a chicken at Common Ground High School in New Haven, CT – a charter school that focuses on "environmental leadership" – where my kids go to summer camp.

❖ The four bodies seen in the water represent the guitar quartet. The possibility that there are only two bodies, which are seen from two different directions, represent the idea that I played all four parts, duplicating myself.

❖ The sun is a reference to the "sun guitar" on the cover of *The Art of Modern Primitive Guitar*.

BIBLIOGRPAHY

Bach, J.S. *The Well-Tempered Clavier.* G. Schirmer, Inc., 2006 Edition

Barnes, Mike *Captain Beefheart: The Biography.* Cooper Square Press, 2002

Bernstein, Leonard. *The Symphonic Dances of West Side Story.* Boosey & Hawkes, 2004 Edition

Blum, David. *The Art of Quartet Playing: The Guarneri Quartet In Conversation with David Blum.* Cornell University Press, 1987

Brouwer, Leo. *Estudos Sencillos.* Chester Music, 2003

Bruser, Madeline *The Art of Practicing.* Three Rivers Press, 1997

Cage, John. *Sonatas and Interludes for Prepared Piano.* Edition Peters, 1960

Carcassi, Matteo *Classical Guitar Method, Op. 59 & 25 Melodious and Progressive Studies for the Guitar, Op. 60* edited by Bertaud, Philippe. Carl Fischer, 2011

Cohen, Patricia. "Arts as Antidote for Academic Ills." *The New York Times.* December 18, 2012

Cutler, Chris. *File Under Popular.* Autonomedia, 1993 Edition

Dali, Salvador. *Diary of a Genius.* Solar Books, 2006 Edition

Drummond, Bill. *45.* Abacus, 2009

———— *$20,000.* Beautiful Books Limited, 2010

Eno, Brian. *A Year With Swollen Appendices: Brian Eno's Diary.* Faber & Faber, 1996

Everett, Walter. *The Beatles as Musicians.* Oxford University Press, 1999

French, John. *Beefheart: Though The Eyes Of Magic.* Proper Music Publishing Limited, 2013

Frith, Simon and Horne, Howard. *Pop Into Art*. Methuen & Co., 1987

Gordy, Berry. *To Be Loved*. Warner Books, 1994

Greenberg, Robert. *Bach and the High Baroque*. The Great Courses, 2013

———— *How to Listen to and Understand Great Music, 3rd Edition*. The Great Courses, 2013

Harkleroad, Bill *Lunar Notes*. SAF Publishing Ltd., 1998

Higgs, John. *The KLF: Chaos, Magic And The Band Who Burned A Million Pounds*. Phoenix, 2012

Kaku, Michio *Physics of the Future*. Doubleday, 2011

Keillor, Garrison. *Local Man Moves To The City*. HighBridge Audio, 2005

Kirkpatrick, Ralph. *Interpreting Bach's Well-Tempered Clavier*. Yale University Press, 1984

LeRoy, Dan. *The Beastie Boys' Paul's Boutique (33 1/3)*. Bloomsbury Academic, 2006

Mailer, Norman. *Portrait of Picasso as a Young Man*. Abacus, 1997

Nachmanovitch, Stephen. *Free Play*. Jeremy P. Tarcher/ Putnam, 1990

Norton, M.D. Herter. *The Art of String Quartet Playing*. W.W. Notron & Company Ltd., 1962

Persinger, Shawn. *The 50 Greatest Guitar Books*. Quixotic Music, 2013

Persinger, Shawn and Shultz, Tom. *I'm An Alligator. I'm a Crocodile*. Quixotic Music, 2014

Seneca, Lucius Annaeus. *On Benefits: Addressed to Aebutius Liberalis*. George Bell and Sons, 1900

Shahn, Ben. *The Shape Of Content*. Harvard University Press, 1985 Edition

Siblin, Eric. *The Cello Suites: J.S. Bach, Pablo Casals, and the Search for a Baroque Masterpiece.* Grove Press 2009

Sor, Fernando. *The Complete Studies, Lessons, and Exercises for Guitar* edited by Jeffery, Brian. Tecla, 2008 Edition

Stravinsky, Igor. *The Firebird Suite.* Dover Publications, 1987

Tamm, Eric. *Brian Eno: His Music And The Vertical Color Of Sound.* Da Capo Press, 1995

Wikipedia contributors. "Trait theory." Wikipedia, The Free Encyclopedia, July 27, 2016

Zorn, John (Editor). *Arcana.* Hips Road/Tzadik, 2000

N/A. *The Quotable Traveler: Wise Words For Travelers, Explorers, And Wanderers.* Running Press, 1994

ABOUT THE AUTHOR

Shawn Persinger began his musical career in 1991 after graduating from Musicians Institute in Los Angeles, CA. Since that time, he has been featured in *Relix, Jazziz, The Village Voice, Gramophone, Guitar World*, and many other publications. In 2004, *Acoustic Guitar* magazine named his solo album *The Art of Modern Primitive Guitar* one of the best CDs of the year. His acoustic duo, Prester John, had their album *Desire for a Straight Line* included on the 2010 Grammy nomination ballot for "Best Contemporary Jazz Recording", and his 1990s progressive band Boud Deun is still cited as one of the standouts of the genre, with *The Billboard Guide To Progressive Rock* listing their *Astronomy Made Easy* as one of the 30 Best-Sounding [Progressive] Recordings of all time.

As a music educator Persinger has taught thousands of students and directed multifarious ensembles and group workshops. He has served on the faculty at Guitar Intensives in Bar Harbor, ME; The Center for Creative Youth in Middletown, CT; and The National Guitar Workshop in Nashville, TN. He is currently an adjunct lecturer at The University of New Haven in New Haven, CT.

ABOUT THE ILLUSTRATOR

Gonzalo Fuentes Riquelme is a Chilean artist who has spent most of his life teaching himself to draw, paint, and play music. In addition to creating art for art's sake, Gonzalo has contributed illustrations to several album and book covers. He also conducts a variety of artistic workshops, lectures on contemporary art, performs live music, and spends time producing eclectic radio programs.

In 2017 Gonzalo produced *Frets Of Yore*, an international, multimedia compilation CD and visual arts project featuring the music of Fred Frith, Henry Kaiser, Amy Denio Elliot Sharp, et al., as well as the art of Jad Fair, Danielle Dax, Cal Schenkel, Matt Howarth, and many others. He is currently producing a similar project for release in 2018.

GUERRILLA GRAPHICS

For more information please visit: www.guerrillagraphics.cl